FARRELL'S ICE CREAM PARLOUR RESTAURANTS

Copyright © Farrell's 1966-1975

Farrell's Ice Cream Parlours

Copyright © 2024 by Gerald E. "Jerry" Naftaly

JerryNaftaly.com

All rights reserved. No part of this book may be reproduced or transmitted in any form or by any means without written permission from the author.

ISBN 978-0-9980352-7-7
Printed in USA 48 Hour Books

Dedication

I proudly dedicate this book to my parents, Bill and Grace Naftaly, of blessed memory. They taught me the value of kindness, the importance of listening, the worth of friendship, of preserving and sharing history, and of public service.

This book is also dedicated to Bob Farrell for his vision of an old-fashioned ice cream parlour for the whole family to enjoy. Furthermore, it is dedicated to everyone who shared in preserving the legacy of Bob Farrell, including those who played a part in the success of the business, either as a customer, an employee, a manager, or as an owner.

Farrell's Timeline Highlights

1963 - Bob Farrell and Ken McCarthy founded Farrell's.

1965 – The second Farrell's opened. The Franchise was in Salem, Oregon.

1966 – The second company-owned Farrell's opened in Portland, Oregon.

1968 - John Ortman built the first store in La Mesa. He then built seven locations in the San Diego County area and he was the most successful and longest franchisee.

1968 – New franchised stores were awarded in Michigan, Hawaii, and other states. Farrell's also arrived in Scottsdale, Arizona.

1970 - Ken McCarthy retired from Farrell's. Hawaii opens.

1971 – Farrell's goes international and opened a location in British Columbia.

1972 - Marriott acquires Farrell's in a stock deal.

1975 – Farrell's opens its 100th location - Tampa, Florida.

1976 - High Water Mark - 92 corporate owned and 23 franchised locations, plus 2 "others."

1978 – Farrell's returned to profitability - first time in 3 years.

1979 – Seattle, Southcenter Mall – First location to reach $1 million in sales!

1981/1982 – A private investor's group bought Farrell's from Marriott for $15 million.

1982 – 74 company-owned, 31 franchised, and 2 specialty locations.

1983 – The company revamped the menu and eliminated the siren and bell.

1985 – Marriott started to provide management services - shifts focus to selling stores.

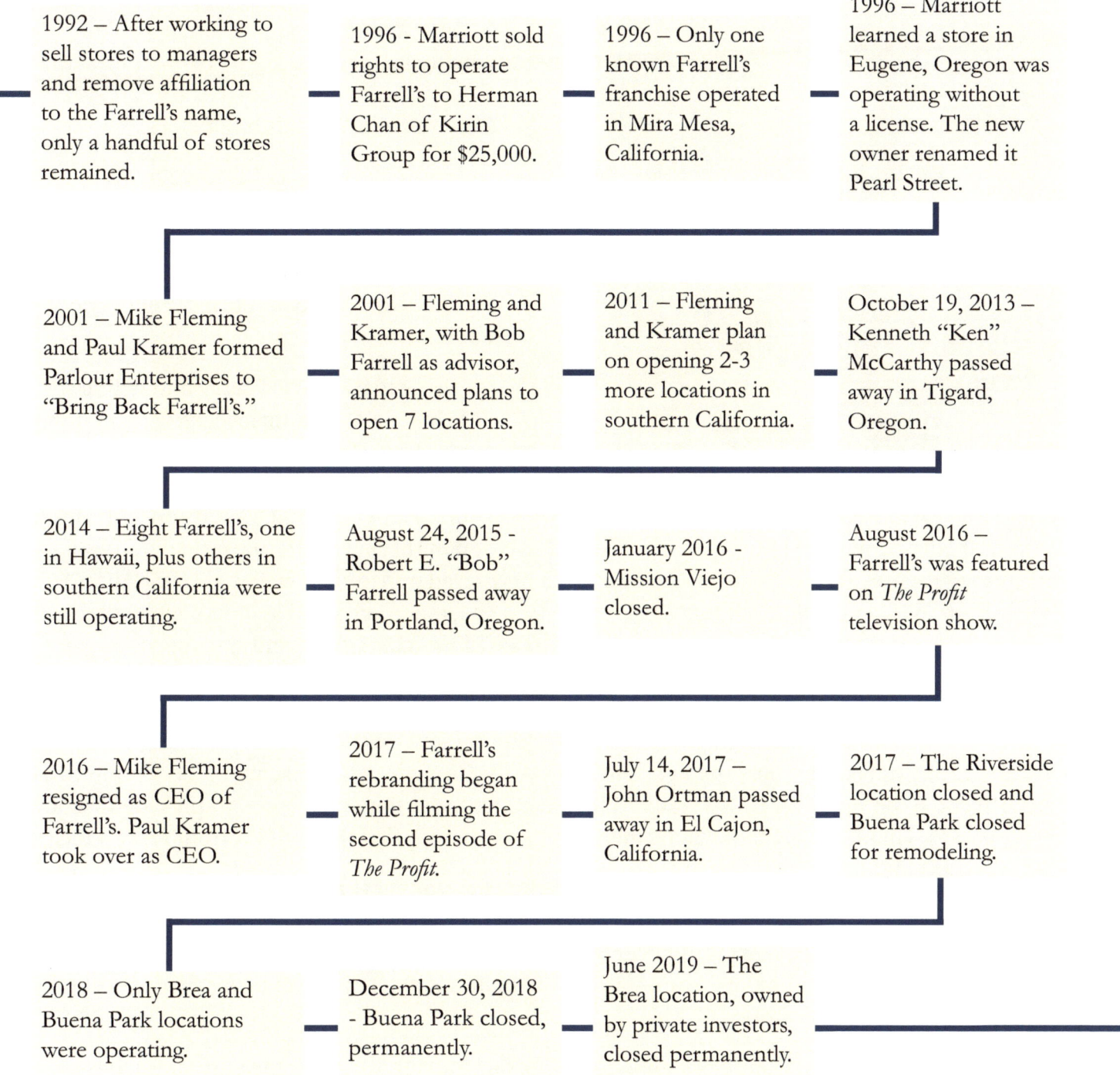

1992 – After working to sell stores to managers and remove affiliation to the Farrell's name, only a handful of stores remained.

1996 - Marriott sold rights to operate Farrell's to Herman Chan of Kirin Group for $25,000.

1996 – Only one known Farrell's franchise operated in Mira Mesa, California.

1996 – Marriott learned a store in Eugene, Oregon was operating without a license. The new owner renamed it Pearl Street.

2001 – Mike Fleming and Paul Kramer formed Parlour Enterprises to "Bring Back Farrell's."

2001 – Fleming and Kramer, with Bob Farrell as advisor, announced plans to open 7 locations.

2011 – Fleming and Kramer plan on opening 2-3 more locations in southern California.

October 19, 2013 – Kenneth "Ken" McCarthy passed away in Tigard, Oregon.

2014 – Eight Farrell's, one in Hawaii, plus others in southern California were still operating.

August 24, 2015 - Robert E. "Bob" Farrell passed away in Portland, Oregon.

January 2016 - Mission Viejo closed.

August 2016 – Farrell's was featured on *The Profit* television show.

2016 – Mike Fleming resigned as CEO of Farrell's. Paul Kramer took over as CEO.

2017 – Farrell's rebranding began while filming the second episode of *The Profit*.

July 14, 2017 – John Ortman passed away in El Cajon, California.

2017 – The Riverside location closed and Buena Park closed for remodeling.

2018 – Only Brea and Buena Park locations were operating.

December 30, 2018 - Buena Park closed, permanently.

June 2019 – The Brea location, owned by private investors, closed permanently.

With thanks and appreciation to Roger Baker, Mike Fleming, and Tom Ortman for their input. Information was also obtained from Wikipedia and the ***Give 'Em The Pickle*** book by Bob Farrell and Bill Perkins. Additional information was obtained from the Marriott Corp Annual reports. This information is believed to be reliable and accurate.

ABOUT THE AUTHOR

Gerald (Jerry) E. Naftaly is the long-time Mayor and City Councilman of Oak Park, Michigan. Jerry served 14 years as a City Councilmember, followed by 20 years as Mayor, from 1977 through 2011.

Jerry earned his BS Degree at Wayne State University, Detroit, Michigan, with a major in accounting and a minor in marketing. He worked at his family's CPA firm, Geller Naftaly, for 11 years during high school and college.

This experience led Jerry into public service and his first, but unsuccessful, run for city council in 1975. While working at the CPA firm he was elected to city council two years later, in 1977. Next, Jerry took his lifelong interest in the stock market to become a registered investment broker in 1979. He had a 30-plus-year career as the vice president of investments and was a registered portfolio manager at UBS/PaineWebber and then Baird & Company. Attending WSU in 1973, a gas and oil crisis developed, which led to long lines at the pump with "odd & even' days to purchase gas. Jerry envisioned and spearheaded a park and ride shuttle bus service leaving Oak Park and taking riders to Wayne State and downtown Detroit. He organized discussions with WSU, the Southeast Michigan Transportation Authority (SEMTA), and the city. Jerry was successful in bringing the service to fruition and, because of its popularity, buses were added at various times, both leaving and returning. City Council then presented a certificate to Jerry for his efforts. Even his Dad, Bill Naftaly volunteered and met the early buses to provide discounted SEMTA passes. Hundreds of students, faculty, shoppers, and workers benefitted from Jerry's idea.

When elected to the City Council in 1977, Jerry was the youngest member in the city's history. He was re-elected in 1979, 1983, and 1987 serving for 14 consecutive years. Then, in November 1991, the retiring Mayor endorsed Jerry. He became the youngest Oak Park Mayor in the first of ten, two-year terms. Jerry is proud of his 34 years serving the community, as well as being the longest serving member of Oak Park's City Council.

For his distinguished and exemplary public service, on October 30, 2013, the City Council issued the following proclamation. "In honor of his dedication and commitment to the City and for the countless hours he worked to see the municipal complex, including the City Hall, Public Safety, and District Court, become a reality, we hereby dedicate the *Gerald E. Naftaly Municipal Complex*."

Jerry, a long-time fan, is shown here with a variety of Farrell's items which were contributed by Mike Fleming, Dick Erb, Bill Perkins, and Media Partners/Atana.

Jerry has authored three books: *Images of Oak Park* (2012), *Images of Northland Mall* (2016), *The Hill That Grew* (2019), and Second Editions of *The Hill* and of *Northland Mall*. Several have won Finalist book awards.

Photo (C) Elayne Gross Photography

Farrell's Ice Cream Parlours

Jerry Naftaly

Contents

Timeline Highlights ....i-ii
Acknowledgements 11
Introduction 13

    1. Bob Farrell and Family 15
    2. The Birth of Farrell's 23
    3. Key Players of Farrell's 29
    4. Farrell's Restaurants Across America 43
    5. Farrell's Fountain Menu 57
    6. History of The Farrell's Menus 67
    7. Birthday Parties and Family Fun 87
    8. The People – Employees and Customers 97
    9. Activities and VIPs 103
  10. From Tragedy Comes Help and Hope 113
  11. The Marriott Years 121
  12. Marcus Lemonis *"The Profit"* TV Show
       The Auction of Memorabilia 127

Acknowledgements

Writing about Farrell's Ice Cream Parlours was possible due to the collaboration and contributions of friends, and those closely involved with the business. Photographs, historical context, and fond memories of this era were shared in order to complete the book. It would not have been attainable without their involvement.

Thank you to Mike Fleming, Roger Baker, Paul Kramer, Tom Ortman and his late father, John Ortman, of blessed memory. Thank you, Bill Perkins, co-author of *Give 'Em The Pickle* and creator of the training programs and seminars. Thanks to the late Dr. Henry Brandt and his children, Dick, Suzanne, and Beth. Thank you, Ramona "Mona" Farrell, Dick and Kristie Farrell Booster. Thank you for sharing Bob Farrell with all of us!

Thank you, Dwight Manley, Jeff Dunham, Matt McNeil, and Robert Hartmann. I appreciate the conversations I had with Dick and Kay Erb, and Dick's recollections of Farrell's, and Marriott. Thank you, Marcus Lemonis, your staff, and your production company. Thanks, also to NBC/Universal and specifically Tom Ekelman, Jessica Brenner, and Chuck Brewer for their kind assistance with images from *The Profit* show. Thanks to publicist Donn Pearlman and Shannon Watson for Dwight Manley's biographical information and Brea photographs on behalf of Mr. Manley. Thank you, Bobby Gerber, for your time and assistance.

Thank you, Hon. Jennifer Granholm, United States Secretary of Energy, and former Governor of Michigan, for sharing your story about working for Farrell's as a teenager.

Thank you to my friends and family who have supported me by reading my chapters and offering suggestions, encouragement, or questions. Thank you, Harold and Iris Mickel, Mike and Kim Soave, Jim and Diane Luxton, Alan H. Kideckel, Aaron Tobin, Emile J. Duplessis, Paul and Sharon Landau Levine, Randy and Heidi Press Carr, Bob and Robin Gershman, Bob and Karen Seifert, Bill Molner, and Jeffrey Markowitz. Special thanks to Judi Markowitz for her detailed revisions and for providing a needed, critical review. Thanks to Elayne Gross for her photographic skills and expertise. Love you, Lisa Naftaly Brown and Howard Brown, my niece and nephew.

Thank you to the many friends who shared their stories and photographs. Thank you, Jon Nachman for your photographs and the large Farrell's poster. Thank you, Aaron Schwartz, Bob Solomon, Jeff and Jan Zorn, Doug Amaro, Andy Schulist, Richard I. Weiss, Bill Molner, and more.

Thank you to Katie Dishman, Corporate Archivist of Marriott International. Thank you to John Guest of Christophers, Inc. and their president, David Nierodzinski. Thanks to Amy Stark, Jeff Patterson, Tari Blalock, and Johan Graham of i15 Auctions.

Thank you, Rachel Crowell, Director of the Firefighters Burn Institute, Sacramento, California.

Lastly, thank you to Atana, formerly Media Partners, especially Lyndi Calder and Tom Matthews for their generous time and assistance in providing Bob's Pickle marketing and training material.

Introduction

You may have been one of those kids whose parents took you to Farrell's for a free sundae and to hear a group of people singing happy birthday to you.

You may have joined friends attending a birthday party and you got to eat one of the biggest ice cream sundaes you ever saw - "The Zoo!"

Maybe you made a pig of yourself at Farrell's.

You may have been one of the thousands of employees who were part of an iconic ice cream parlour that made people, of all ages, happy and excited.

If any of these memories come to light, you'll want to explore these pages in detail.

It all started with the vision of Bob Farrell. It then continued with a partnership that was formed with Ken McCarthy to create some unique and festive fountain and food treats.

It evolved into a business philosophy and training program like no other, when Bob Farrell teamed with Bill Perkins to write the book, *Give 'Em The Pickle,* and then create business presentations. It expanded even more with Media Partners to produce videos and training material. It wasn't just having a great product. They took their product to a higher level in order to educate others about the values of great customer service.

And they succeeded!

Say the words "Farrell's Ice Cream Parlours" and you're taken back to "The Gay 90's" when everything was focused on having fun. The staff even greeted customers when they walked in.

In this book, you'll get a peek into "The Zoo," the "Pig's Trough," and other fountain favorites, and how they were created.

You'll be reminded of birthday party memories and being singled out in front of friends and strangers. You will be taken in a Time Machine where VIP's and celebrities wanted to be part of the Farrell's traditions.

You'll share in the menus with all the splendiferous concoctions and parties for any reason, whatsoever.

You'll be taken on an adventure to some of the 130 or so Farrell's that served us across the country along with some unique stories…

There were several tragedies and sadly, people died because of two plane crashes and a car accident. However, some good came out of that through the efforts of generous people.

You'll be able to view part of the television show that first caught my attention in August 2016 to see that Farrell's was still prospering after all these years.

Even though it was short-lived, after the television show episodes had aired, I was glad to have a taste of it again, despite the changes from its early beginnings.

As the end became apparent after the closure of one of the last locations, I was able to buy some pieces of the Farrell's history in a national auction.

Along the way, on my voyage that I share with you, I was able to meet many fascinating and amazing people who wanted to keep the legacy of Bob Farrell alive.

I think we are all better off for having participated in the Farrell's business model and "Give 'Em The Pickle" philosophy.

As one of their slogans said, "Farrell's Featured Fabulous Food and Fantastic Fountain Fantasies for Frolicking Fun-Filled Festive Families."

Bob Farrell saw something that was missing, and he succeeded in filling that void. Thank you, Bob Farrell for providing us the enjoyment and the Farrell's name for more than 50 years!

Bob Farrell and Family

Mr. Robert "Bob" Farrell was born December 10, 1927, in Brooklyn, New York. "After his father's untimely death when he was 4 years old, he and his sister were placed in a church run children's home in Yonkers, New York. They remained there for five years until his mother remarried and was able to reassume responsibility for their care. He often said, "I cried when I went in, and I cried when I had to leave." Bob "joined the U.S. Air Force in 1945. While stationed at McChord Field in Washington State, he met his future wife, Ramona "Mona" Rod, in a chance encounter at a local dance." They married in July 1951 and raised three daughters: Kathy, Kristie, and Colleen. Bob did not graduate from high school, but said he received his G.E.D. or "Good Enough Diploma," as he referred to it. He later "found his calling and went on to graduate from Packard College in New York and the University of Washington, earning degrees in business and marketing. Bob was a salesman for Libby McNeill in Seattle and Walla Walla, WA, and transferred to Portland in 1961." (Published by The Oregonian.)

Photo of Bob Farrell from his book, *Give 'Em The Pickle.*

"In 1963, Bob opened his first Farrell's Ice Cream Parlor with business partner, Kenneth McCarthy. He had two goals in mind: keep the customers smiling and provide employees with fun and rewarding work. Farrell's was one of the fastest growing restaurants of its time. Later, Bob became a partner of Pacific Coast Restaurants and helped build a string of Stanford's and Newport Bay restaurants in Oregon, Washington, and Northern California. In 1995, Farrell left the restaurant business and provided customer service consultation to companies like Nordstrom's, Nike, and Safeway. His service training model, "Give 'em the Pickle," is still used today across several industries. Bob loved the Lord. He never shied away from letting people know that the source of his hope and strength came from Jesus Christ. He combined his love of fun, faith and helping young people by becoming involved in Young Life Ministries. Some of the best weeks of his life were spent at Malibu, in Canada, working with the camp's crews. Of all his accomplishments though, family was his priority. As a husband, father and grandfather, he was intentional and intentionally fun. He was personally humble, but loudly proud of his family. He highly valued getting everyone together for any occasion, including road trips, river-rafting adventures, numerous weeks at family camp and holidays at the beach. He loved making us laugh and always pointed us to Jesus, giving Him all the credit." (According to Bob Farrell's obituary, Published by The Oregonian.)

Tributes honoring the memory of Bob Farrell came in from across the country. These comments were posted on the funeral home website:

"I was honored to have known Bob for the many years I did. He was a mentor to me as he was to so many. His distinctive voice I hear from time-to-time when I see his photo in my office… his memory lives in so many of those he touched. God Bless him." – *Mike F.*

"A visionary. One of the best times of my life was spent at the South Center Farrell's Ice cream Parlor Restaurants with three ARMY buddies and my family. Thanks for the memories. Rest in Peace "Bob" Farrell. Job WELL done." – *Dave*

"Bob Farrell, you, and your ice cream parlors will always live in our hearts and memories. Thank you for the gift of so many happy occasions there. Praying for God's comfort for your entire family." – *Barbara B.*

"We celebrated birthday after birthday at the Whittwood Mall Farrells in Whittier, CA. My brothers, sister, and I are all in our 50's now and whenever we think about our childhood, we think about Farrells. We talk about the Zoo, the sirens, and the employees running it around the restaurant…. I made a pig of myself at Farrells. Rest in peace Bob." – *Carrie*

"I remember listening to Bob deliver his story to a group of store managers at Safeway in the early 90's. What a wonderful storyteller. You could tell he had a way with people. You could tell he was humble. I remember his presentation 20 plus years later. God bless him and your family." – *Dave M.*

"I was a cashier in Beaumont, Texas. God bless your family. I truly loved working there. Rest in paradise, Mr. Farrell." – *Ruby*

"I worked at the Farrell's Ice Cream Parlor in Torrance, Ca. for 3 years when it first opened. I met my future husband… I have great memories from that time…Thank you, Mr. Farrell. Sending prayers and peace to the family. I'm sure he is missed." -*Ellen M.*

"Such a sad time for family and friends. I remember when we had a Farrells in Troy MI, by Oakland Mall. It was always a happy place to go as a young child, especially when it was your birthday. You will be deeply missed." – *Michelle K.*

The Farrell family pose with the company car. From left to right are Kristie, Colleen, Bob, Ramona, and Kathy. The dog's name is Albert. (Circa 1968 Courtesy of the Farrell's family.)

I asked Bob and Mona's daughter and son-in-law, Kristie and Dick Booster, to describe Bob Farrell, and Kristie offered this description of her father, "Bob Farrell was a man of integrity. He loved his family well. He believed in hard work and made work a positive experience. Above all, he knew God was guiding his life and was thankful to Him for all he had and experienced. When someone said thank you to Bob, he always replied, 'Thank the Lord.'"

Bob and Mona Farrell at the rear of the car in front of the Marriott Hotel registration entrance.

Bob Farrell as a Keystone cop.

Bob Farrell as a young man.
(Courtesy of Mike Fleming.)

Bob Farrell on the Merv Griffin Show.
(Courtesy of Mike Fleming.)

Bob Farrell gives the Peace sign while standing next to the symbol of his "Give 'Em The Pickle".
(Courtesy I-15 Auctions.)

In 1976, Bob Farrell was one of 14 Americans presented with the Horatio Alger Award at the 29th Annual Awards program at New York's Waldorf Astoria. The Award was presented "for personifying the realization of the American dream of opportunity and achievement." Bob Farrell is standing, second row, far right. Also pictured are recipients Art Linkletter, radio and television personality, standing second row, far left, and Rod McKuen, best-selling poet, singer-songwriter, and composer, fourth row far left, with beard. Committee President George Shinn is seated, third from left. Art Linkletter was Canadian-born and became a naturalized United States citizen in 1942. (Courtesy of the Farrell's family.)

Bob and Mona pose next to the plaque at Brea. It reads he received the award "because of Bob's hard work, dedication, and creativity, his vision has become a source of fun-tastic lifetime memories for tens of millions of guests across the United States, and in appreciation of his lasting vision and philosophy of always doing our best for our guests and cast members." – 2012 (Courtesy, Mike Fleming.)

Bob and Mona Farrell recreate the famous, iconic Farrell's Ice Cream Parlours logo. With their favorite Farrell's sodas, Bob and Mona share a tender moment in the Brea, California restaurant, 2012, one year after the opening.

A Celebration of Life honoring Bob Farrell was held on September 13, 2015, at the New Heights Church.

Of all his accomplishments though, family was his priority. As a husband, father and grandfather, he was intentional and intentionally fun. He was personally humble, but loudly proud of his family. He highly valued getting everyone together for any occasion, including road trips, river-rafting adventures, numerous weeks at family camp and holidays at the beach. He loved making us laugh and always pointed us to Jesus, giving Him all the credit. We will miss his kind words, thoughtful notes and steadfast support.

Attending the Celebration of Life service to honor Bob Farrell are, from left, Sandy Gruzdis, Cathy Nail, Paul Kramer, Travis Lee, Max Werderman, Mike Fleming. (Courtesy of Mike Fleming.)

You can honor the memory of Bob Farrell with a contribution to:
Dementia Society of America. DementiaSociety.org
Young Life, Prescott, AZ; YoungLife.org
Or a Charity of your choice.

The Birth of Farrell's

This book, *Give 'Em The Pickle,* written by Robert E. Farrell with Bill Perkins, is based on the "principles of leadership, teamwork, and customer service" that evolved out of running "157 successful restaurants" and would become the basis of Bob's successful motivational seminars. What follows are some of the lessons that Bob says he learned "from a lifetime of experiences, and a lifetime of relationships." In the book, Bob credits those who helped in the success of Farrell's Ice Cream Parlours.

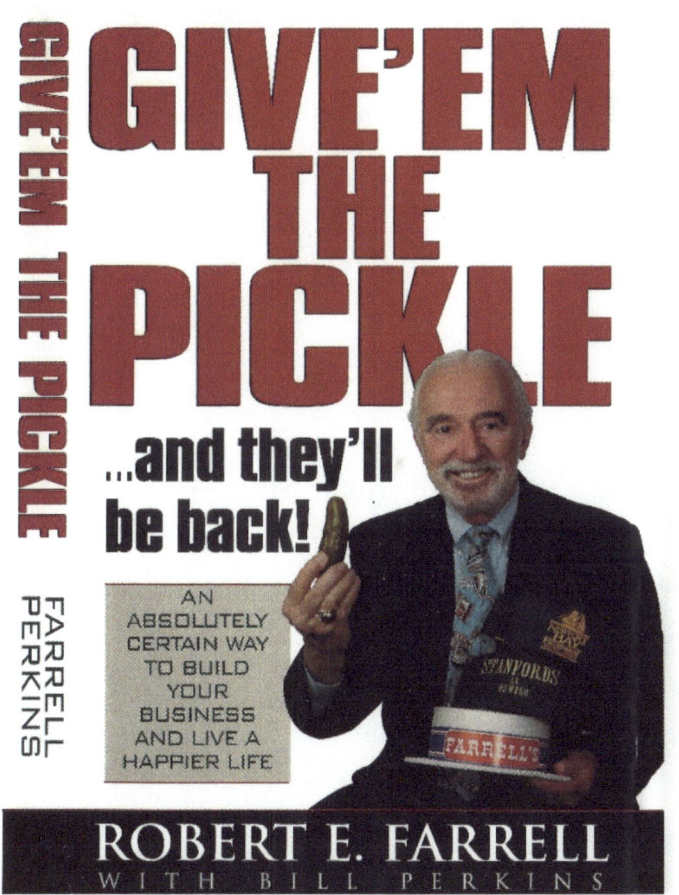

Bob Farrell describes an incident in his book under the heading "The Birth of Farrell's Ice Cream Parlours" when Bob and his wife, Mona, were in Seattle one Sunday afternoon. "I was dying for a hot-fudge sundae and Mona and I could not think of a single place in Seattle where we could get good ice cream on a Sunday afternoon. Finally, I remembered that the Olympic Hotel had served delicious hot-fudge sundaes at a banquet I'd attended.

I rounded up the kids, piled them into the car, and headed for Seattle. Once in a plush red booth in the dining room of the Hotel, the waiter asked, "What will you have today?" Bob replied "We would like five hot-fudge sundaes. We've already had dinner, and we're starved for ice cream. The waiter silently stared at me, lifted his chin, and disdainfully asked, "Is that all you want?"

Bob said, "Immediately something exploded inside of me. The tone of his voice implied we had committed a social crime by ordering an inexpensive dish in his plush restaurant. I kept my cool, but it wasn't easy." Bob Farrell would go on to say he turned to Mona as they were walking out of the motel, and he said, "Why on earth do waiters treat customers so poorly? Don't they realize customers like me are the key to their success?" Bob noted he had entertained as many as two hundred people during grocery trade meetings at that hotel. The decision he made at that moment would change his life. And I note, the lives of many others. "I told Mona, there aren't any good ice cream parlours in Seattle – Nice places where families are treated right no matter what they order. I swear, I'm going to start one!" The rest is history. We are grateful, Bob Farrell!

THE PICKLE PRINCIPLE

Bob Farrell's idea for giving pickles away came from the following letter.

Dear Mr. Farrell,

I've been coming to your restaurant for over three years. I always order a #2 hamburger and a chocolate shake. I always ask for an extra pickle and I always get one. Mind you, this has been going on once or twice a week for three years.

I came into your restaurant the other day and I ordered my usual #2 hamburger and a chocolate shake. I asked the young waitress for an extra pickle. I believe she was new because I hadn't seen her before. She said, "Sir, I will sell you a side of pickles for $1.25." I told her, "No, I just want one extra slice of pickle. I always ask for it and they always give it to me. Go ask your manager."

She went away and came back after speaking to the manager. The waitress looked me in the eye and said, "I'll sell you a pickle for a nickel." Mr. Farrell, I told her what to do with her pickle, hamburger, and milkshake. I'm not coming back to your restaurant if that's the way you're going to run it.

Bob would describe what he did after reading the letter.

"He signed his name and, fortunately for me, included his address. I wrote him a letter and enclosed a card for a free hot fudge sundae. I assured him we don't run our business that way, apologized, and asked him to please come back. I had a chance meeting with him years later and I thanked him in person for his letter because it became the "war cry" of our young company, "Give 'em the Pickle." When something happens with a customer and you're not sure what to do? "Give 'em the Pickle!" Do what it takes to make things right!" The pickle philosophy has evolved as it has been put into practice at various businesses. It may be about going the extra mile to make customers happy or putting your own personal stamp on customer service that sets you apart from your competition. At my favorite tire store, they literally run to greet me when I step out of my car in the parking lot. I've met garbage collectors who stop to start lawn mowers and coffee baristas who add a heart or other designs in the latte foam. Those are all pickles. What are yours?"

"IS THAT ALL YOU ARE HAVING?"

"YOU ARE HERE TO SERVE ME, THE CUSTOMER, THE BOSS!"

The drawing at left depicts how Bob was made to feel. Depicted at right, as a child, Bob credits his mother "with the greatest lesson in retail sales: THE CUSTOMER IS THE BOSS!" From Bob Farrell's book.

Mr. Bob Farrell inspired those around him as he founded the ice cream parlours that bore his name. However, he wouldn't stop at just his employees, other Parlour executives, staff, and guests. Farrell would go on to inspire and train hundreds of other company executives and their employees with his lectures and presentations.

Bill Perkins co-wrote the book with Bob Farrell and helped take it to the next level. Before the book, it started with a speech that Bob Farrell had written. It was "Give 'em the Pickle." Bill and Bob would meet to discuss Bob's speech and the potential for a book. However, Bill Perkins wanted to develop it into something more. Bill envisioned a half-day seminar to help train business employees about customer service. What resulted was not only the book, but training videos and programs that would educate as well as motivate.

Combining with Media Partners between 1997 and 2007, Bob Farrell would produce videos and inspirational marketing materials based on his "Give 'em the Pickle" philosophy. Bob spent subsequent years sharing his business philosophy across the country. Domino's Pizza of Ann Arbor and the Oregon State Police were just two of the diversified clientele.

"Bob Farrell taught that great companies and successful employees do 4 things:"

Service - Make serving others your number one priority.

Attitude - How you think about customers is how you will treat them.

Consistency - Set high service standards and live by them every day.

Teamwork - Look for ways to make each other look good.

This package of video, book, and handouts are available from Atana.

Bob Farrell's famous quote in his book, *The Leadership Pickles,* with Michele Eby:

"If our employees are not better people for having worked for us, then we have failed."

The Leadership Pickles will inspire your employees to follow you and achieve great things.

Spread **Enthusiasm**
Inspire **Confidence**
Demonstrate **Integrity**

Media Partners, now known as Atana, continues to provide valuable training to organizations to help inspire management and employees. They have provided multi-award-winning training programs for decades. Bob Farrell's books and videos, shown in the images on these pages, are still available for purchase. For further information, please contact Media Partners/Atana at www.Atana.com There is a "Live Chat" and "Contact Us" form available. Thanks to Atana for their permission to use the copyrighted images and information from their training material.

The Bob Farrell Bobblehead was a gift to me from Dick Erb. He presented it to me knowing it was going to someone who would value it, and I do. Thank you, Dick Erb! This is a special gift! I hope that you are proud of this book, the preservation of the memories of Farrell's, and the important part you played in the history of this wonderful company!

Bob Farrell described the "pickle" as "something special you do for the customer. It's a little something extra that sets your business apart. Maybe it's a handwritten note in a shipment or using the customer's name. Every business has its own type of pickles to give away. It's just a matter of figuring out what that special something is. At Farrell's it was personal service. It was singing 'Happy Birthday' and giving kids a free sundae on their birthday. It was extra pickles."

Leadership Pickles, according to Bob Farrell, are "the things you do to motivate your employees, to show them you care about them, to help them see what good customer service looks like." Bob's training guides give the "specific, effective strategies for these seven leadership pickles to your employees: "Enthusiasm, Urgency, Confidence, Encouragement, Appreciation, Integrity, and Service."

I purchased this memento in the final auction of Farrell's items. It is Farrell's "Mission Statement," listing the company values and standards. "To Deliver Happy-Itis To Every Guest. Every Day." The Ice "CREAM" Standards of **C**are, **R**esponsibility, **E**nthusiasm, **A**bility, **M**aintain Appearance. It is signed by Robert Farrell at the top along with the employees. It is applicable to Everyone. **Jerry Naftaly**

Key Players of Farrell's

3

John C. Ortman (April 14, 1928 – July 14, 2017) was the owner of Farrell's Ice Cream Parlours in San Diego. John was a "legend in the restaurant industry, having built his first Farrell's store in La Mesa in 1968 and subsequently seven more stores throughout San Diego County." John's obituary paid tribute to his life by noting, "he was the most successful franchisee and operated his stores longer than any other owner. His success was due to his passion for bringing a clean, wholesome family restaurant business to San Diego and being involved daily in the business." John Ortman motivated several former employees to open their own businesses and others to become corporate executives. John Ortman served 22 years in the US Navy, retiring as a Lieutenant. The images on the following pages are from the John Ortman collection, courtesy of his son, Tom Ortman.

At left, Bob Farrell and John Ortman are proud owners when the La Mesa store opens. Bottom left, John Ortman's wife Ann talking to John, and Jerry Kellerman, their general manager for all the stores. Below right, L to R, Oliver Lund, John Ortman's initial partner, John's mother Helen Ortman, of blessed memory, and John in the candy shop.

Miss La Mesa, 1967, helps with the ribbon cutting at the grand opening. At right, kneeling and holding the ribbon, is John Ortman with Bob Farrell standing behind him. The man kneeling, at left, is Jerry Kellerman. John and Jerry were Navy "buddies" and John hired him as the general manager of all the Ortman units. As a team, John and Jerry were both dedicated, hard workers who were instrumental in the success of Farrell's in San Diego.

At left, The Ortman management team joins a goal-setting meeting with franchisees in 1968, including a goal of 18 outlets while including their focus on "constant quality."

At right, John Ortman (standing, third from left) and Bob Farrell (standing, far right) join the management team for discussions that included advertising, promotions, and delivering a fun time for all.

L to R, John Zaverski, Oliver Lund, and John Ortman who were two of Ortman's original business partners.

The Farrell's Newsletter, "The Scoop" featuring the second annual convention in Seattle. Thirty-nine men plus Donna Casebolt. Left, the official flag-raising ceremony at the La Mesa location, February 1968. Below, John Ortman, center in both images, and the Padres had a close bond and friendship. John provided many Farrell's ice cream coupons for special events. (Courtesy, Tom Ortman and the Ortman collection.)

ORTMAN SCORES AGAIN IN SAN DIEGO!

Farrell's franchisee John Ortman and his merry band of Farrell's funlovers in San Diego have been given the royal pat-on-the-back from the city's mayor, Pete Wilson.

In a letter to President Bob Farrell, Mayor Wilson said that the Farrell's Do-Gooders recently contributed over $700 in cash, as well as their time and ice cream to the Leukemia Radiothon held there.

The mayor went on to mention that Farrell's-San Diego has also been a recipient of annual awards from the Muscular Dystrophy organization and United Funds, and has been "involved with COMBO, ORT, PTA, Little League, Boys Clubs and most of the charitable and sports functions in this City."

The mayor ended his letter saying "If the San Diego involvement is indicative of your organization, you not only have a great thing going, but are doing **great things!**"

Thank you, Mr. Mayor, for your kind words (blush.) And THANK YOU, John Ortman and the Farrell's gang down in sunny San Diego, for doing such a SUPERIFIC job!!!!!

In the spring of 1974, then-mayor of San Diego, Pete Wilson, gave the "royal pat-on-the-back" to Farrell's and both Bob Farrell and John Ortman. The company, Bob and John were honored for supporting many charities in the San Diego area. Farrell's and, specifically the San Diego units managed by John Ortman, were recognized by many of the local charities and sports programs in the community. Mayor Pete Wilson would serve from 1971 to 1983, then as U.S Senator from 1983 to 1991, and lastly as the 36th governor of California from 1991 to 1999. (From the John Ortman collection.)

John Ortman was personally involved in the success of his Farrell's franchise. He actively participated in the operations, and even listed his home phone number on his card.

Dwight Manley sent these photos to me and noted, "that picture is of me at 4 years old. I never worked at Farrell's. I was just a big fan growing up and loved the nostalgia." Dwight Manley is the Managing Partner of Manley Fanticola Partners in Brea, California. He is a professional numismatist (his interest began at the age of six when he received a 1909 Lincoln cent). He is a successful real estate developer and former sports agent. Ironically, this same 4-year-old would grow up to own the location of the Farrell's in Brea, including several buildings that contain shops and apartments. Manley recruited them to open their Brea location and continues to own the building today.

In 1999, Manley made the world's largest numismatic purchase by acquiring the $100 million-plus California Gold Rush sunken treasure recovered from the legendary 1857 voyage of the S.S. *Central America*, the fabled "Ship of Gold." (Dwight Manley's bio.)

Below right, Dwight Manley and Bob Farrell, center, flanked by Mike Fleming at left, Brea Mayor Don Schweitzer, and Paul Kramer, far right. Below left, Dwight Manley, Mayor Schweitzer, Bob Farrell, Fleming, and Kramer by the Brea entrance. (Courtesy of Mr. Manley.)

Brea Farrell's at night. Photo by Robert Solomon.

Dick Erb, seated on the left with Dr. Henry Brandt, was the General Manager of Farrell's Michigan region and franchisee. Standing behind them is Dick's assistant, Ruth Golden, who supervised their office for the entire time Dick Erb was associated with Farrell's. When Bob Farrell sold the Farrell's chain to Marriott Corp in 1972, Marriott insisted that Dick Erb stay on to continue to oversee operations. Therefore, Dick became the last person to sell his units to Marriott.

Dick reflected that the Southfield and Troy, Michigan stores were the top two locations in the chain. He recalled that the Troy, Oakland Mall location set a record (at that time) by singing "Happy Birthday" 124 times in an eight-hour shift.

The Michigan stores were originally franchised by Dick Erb and Dr. Henry Brandt. Dick initially worked at General Motors in Flint and that would be one of the first locations. The store in Pontiac became a florist shop.

During conversations with Mr. Erb, he reminisced about his time with Farrell's. He talked about the Senior Management positions he held with several major corporations but said, "I have never enjoyed myself more than when I was involved with Farrell's. Bob and I became close friends after we had built three of the Michigan units. When traveling together to conferences, Bob would talk about his faith, and the Bible." When he asked Bob what the most important things in his life were, Bob would be quick to answer, "my faith in God." Dick Erb added, "Bob Farrell was on the national Christian speaker's organization and was in demand. Dr. Brandt was a Christian psychologist who spoke to huge conferences all over the world. That is where Bob Farrell met Dr. Brandt."

Dick Erb also talked about another Farrell's franchise. "The two men who had the Washington State franchise were Joe Rutten, and Jack Machlis, and they were one of the first franchises that Farrell had. Joe was very close to Bob and shared many thoughts when getting Farrell's started as a big chain. Joe was also a good friend of mine, and we shared many phone calls. Four months after we sold to Marriott, Joe and I were promoted to Regional VP in the Restaurant Division of Marriott. He had all the Farrell's on the west coast, and I had the Midwest from Michigan to Texas. We attended a 3-day meeting each month in Washington, DC. Two years later I was asked to move to DC and accept more responsibilities but raising a family of four kids in Washington D.C. and hosting Presidents at-large conferences was not in my interest. So, after a few days of thought, we moved to Spokane (the best move I have ever made.)"

Dick would go on to say, "When reading books on success, such as by Rockefeller, when asked what they attributed their success it was to surround themselves with people smarter than themselves. I never forgot that."

The Grand Opening of the Farrell's in Toledo. Left to right, Bob Farrell, Dick Erb, and Dr. Henry Brandt. While he joined with Dick Erb to help build Farrell's, Dr. Brandt was "a pioneer in Modern-Day Biblical Counseling, His focus was as an international consultant, educator, counselor, author, and conference speaker" said Dr. Brandt's son, Dick, who reflected on his father's main mission in life – that of family living counseling. "He was one of the first to have a radio program devoted to family living. But, through business contacts, he started a chain of buffet restaurants called Sveden House Smorgasbord, one of Michigan's favorite restaurants." (Circa Aug 1971. Photo Courtesy of Dick Erb.)

Dick Brandt talked about the business connections developed by his father who started the chain of Sveden House restaurants. This would lead to meeting Bob Farrell. He recalled driving the family from East Lansing to Frankenmuth for a Zehnder's chicken dinner with Bob Farrell. "That meeting resulted in Bob awarding the rights to build Farrell's in the state of Michigan. Another interesting connection is the fact that my father taught the college age Sunday School at North Baptist Church in Flint. His good friend Mel Willett would go to the General Motors Institute fraternities to invite the fraternity boys to church. So, his Sunday school class was stacked with future General Motors executives. These guys became the managers for Sveden House and Farrell's. Dick Erb was one of those guys." Together, Dick and Dr. Brandt would open eight Farrell's Ice Cream Parlours.

Dick Erb and Farrell's came through on many occasions to benefit organizations and individuals. On one such request in 1974, the Southfield, Michigan Farrell's donated a "10,920-scoop sundae with chocolate topping, sprinkles, and whipped cream, worth over $5,000, to a fund raising for disabled children. Several hundred Boys Club, Boy Scouts, and Boys Republic members participated in the event."

On another occasion, Dick Erb came to the last-minute rescue with the "Ann Arbor outlet providing frozen treats and 18 gallons of ice cream for the W.J. Maxey School, and even offered to send a Farrell's expert scooper to help keep dishes filled," according to the Detroit Free Press.

Farrell's restaurants helped whenever and wherever needed.

The Detroit Free Press offered a column called "Action Line" – and claimed: "It was Michigan's own superhero squad." Readers would call in with problems and the Action Line team would work to solve them. For 15 years, starting in 1966, problems were solved. Farrell's came through on multiple occasions.

Dick Erb and Harold Goldsmith, manager of the Farrell's location on Telegraph Rd, just north of Schoolcraft, threw a party for one hundred underprivileged youngsters, with free food, ice cream, entertainment, and prizes. The Ferndale Co-Op Credit Union picked up the cost of the bus to transport the youngsters. Farrell's donated their time and refreshments.

Roger Baker, above right, with Bob Farrell, started working for Farrell's in 1977 with meager beginnings. Roger held positions in the fountain, kitchen, and he was also a dishwasher. But Roger would quickly move his way up in management with Farrell's, serving in many locations in several states, as his services were needed. Bob Farrell, in the photograph above, was at the Farrell's restaurant in Santa Clarita, California. He was invited to give his "Give 'Em the Pickle" motivational remarks to the owners and management of the location in October 2003. Roger Baker became "lead employee" in Milwaukee in 1982, and then assistant manager a few short months later. Roger was promoted to the Schaumburg and North Riverside, Illinois locations and then, in 1985, was transferred to the Los Angeles region, managing the Torance, California location until it closed. Farrell's would continue to have Roger manage other locations until he took a position with Marriott's hotel division. After more time with other food chains, and as Farrell's was closing locations, Roger Baker would pursue his engineering degree. Roger's brother, Patrick was co-owner of the Brea, California location.

Bob Farrell sold the restaurant chain to Marriott Corporation in 1972. Marriott would sell the remaining stores in 1982 to private investors. This group was led by Richard Blum, chairman of Blum Capital, who was married to Dianne Feinstein from 1980-2022, until his death. Feinstein was Mayor of San Francisco at the time they were married and then a United States Senator until her death in 2023. Their association and some of Blum's investments were not without controversy. There were accusations of conflicts of interest with business dealings and contracts with foreign governments.

The Los Angeles Times reported in 1990 that in 1982, Blum, who "had owned 2,400 shares of Marriott in 1980, had bought from Marriott its struggling chain of Farrell's Ice Cream Parlours for $15 million, $12 million of which was debt. In 1985, after failing to fix the chain, Blum gave it back to Marriott, giving up his original $3-million equity stake plus $1 million more that he had pumped in." The LA Times also reported that, "Blum's and Feinstein's 1985 tax documents show that losses from Farrell's and from the Hotel Carlton, a residential hotel the two own in the city, produced a loss and the couple paid no taxes that year."

Richard Blum at the groundbreaking ceremony for the Blum Center at UC Berkley, 2009. (Jarrett, Wikipedia.)

Pictured, L to R, Paul Kramer, Mike Fleming, Bob Farrell, and Herman Chan. Chan and his corporation, Kirin Group, purchased from Marriott Corporation the rights to develop Farrell's in 1996. Promises and certain understandings were made between the Kirin Group and Parlour Enterprises, owned by Mike Fleming and Paul Kramer. Parlour would ultimately sue Kirin Group for cancelling their Area Development Agreement.

That lawsuit by Parlour Enterprises against Kirin Group sought lost profits, lost franchise fees, and expenses.

The court case noted, "Kirin entered into a series of written agreements with Parlour in 2000 to develop Farrell's subfranchises in California. The agreements consisted of an area development agreement (ADA) and a rider to the ADA. The ADA gave Parlour the exclusive right to subfranchise Farrell's in California…"

Following a month-long trial, court documents showed, "the lawsuit by Parlour against the Kirin Group resulted in a jury award to Parlour for Farrell's of a multimillion-dollar lost profit award. In case summaries and details from the Court of Appeals of California in 2007, based on breach of franchise agreement for three restaurants that Farrell's had specific plans to open but were never established."

In the opinion of the Court, "*Parlour Enterprises, Inc. v. Kirin Group, Inc.*, 152 Cal. App.4th 281, 283-84 (Cal. Ct. App. 2007) ("A jury awarded plaintiffs Parlour Enterprises, Inc. (Parlour), Fun Foods 1, LP (Fun Foods 1), and Fun Foods Block, LP (Fun Foods Block), approximately $6.6 million in damages. The award consisted of lost profits, lost franchise fees, and consequential expenses sustained by plaintiffs. The matter is remanded to the trial court with directions to reduce the award of damages to Parlour to $130,255. In all other respects, the judgment is affirmed.") (June 19, 2007, No. G036525).

"From 1963 to 1972, Bob Farrell opened 55 Farrell's Ice Cream Parlours (Farrell's) around the United States. In 1972, he sold all of them to Marriott Corporation, which opened an additional 85 restaurants. Around 1980, Marriott sold the ice cream parlors, only to take them back three years later. Marriott shut down all Farrell's operations in the mid-1980's, except for a single Farrell's operating in San Diego."

"Chan, who worked at a Farrell's as a teenager, formed Kirin and in 1996 bought the Farrell's trademarks and trade names. In November 1999 he opened a Farrell's in Temecula but closed it in early 2002 because it was not profitable." (Court of Appeal of Ca, Fourth District, Division Three, June 19, 2007.)

Bob Farrell, left, and Bill Perkins with their book.

I had the honor of speaking with Bill Perkins, co-author of the book *Give 'Em the Pickle*, with Bob Farrell. In the book's acknowledgements, Bob Farrell said of Bill: "I want to extend a special thanks to Bill Perkins who pulled this book together. Shortly after Bill and I met, it became obvious we thought alike. Bill has worked in restaurants and is a published author and skilled communicator. He not only took my material and fleshed it out, he added helpful insights and stories. Thanks, Bill." – Bob Farrell.

According to his website Bill Perkins is a "best-selling author who has conducted business and leadership seminars across the country for companies such as Alaska Airlines and McDonald's. Bill has appeared on nationally broadcast radio and television shows."

Bill and I spoke of his early connection with Bob Farrell when Bob wanted to write a book. After an initial interview with Bob's media representatives, a year went by before Bob called Bill to meet for lunch to discuss the book. After he agreed to turn Bob's speech into a book, Bob said, "We'll go 50/50, Perkins." But Bill wanted to do more than author a book.

Bob Farrell had one speech: "Give 'Em the Pickle" that would make a great book. But Bill told Bob he'd like to take his speech and turn it into a half-day customer service and leadership seminar: "Building a Pickle Factory." The idea was to teach companies how to keep their team's pickle jars full, so they'd have pickles to give to customers. Bob told him to put something together and they'll test it with a few local companies. Bill Perkins did that in the Portland, Oregon area, and got "5-star reviews." That's when Bob and Bill became partners, not just with the book but with the best customer service training in the country. Bob would give his speech and Bill would follow.

Bill said, "I had the privilege of traveling the United States with Bob and without a doubt, the company that he and I worked the most with was Auto-Owners Insurance of Lansing, Michigan."

One day, after Bob had given his speech at a hotel in Columbia Gorge, Oregon, he asked Bill, "What can I do to make it better?" Bill noted the story that Bob told in his book of six-year-old Alex (right) whose parents brought him to Farrell's for his birthday. As they were leaving to pay, Bob asked them about their evening. "Fine" was the response, but Bob knew better. Bob persuaded the father to explain what had happened. The man admitted he hadn't told the waiter, just the hostess, that they brought Alex for his free sundae, but most of all for everyone to sing Happy Birthday as they had done with the other kids.

It turned out the hostess forgot to tell the waiter and Alex sat there, without a sundae and listened while other kids were sung to. Bob told the father, "Sir, I'm very sorry." "You ought to be," the father said. With that, Bob lifted the boy onto the counter, grabbed a sundae and handed it to him.

"What's your name," Bob asked. "Alex," he said. "How old are you, Alex?" "I'm six years old" he said with a big smile. Bob turned to everyone in the restaurant and said, "Please turn this way, stop eating, and put your utensils down. We're all going to sing "Happy Birthday" to Alex who is six years old today."

Everybody stood, cheered, and sang for Alex a birthday song he'll never forget. "As Alex's father left, he turned to Bob and said those three magic words, "We'll be back." And Bob Farrell noted "they did come back. It's been over 25 years and they're still coming back. They never forget the fuss we made over Alex."

Bill told me Bob had been telling that story in the middle of his presentations. He said he told Bob, "It's the emotional climax of the speech. Use it as your conclusion." A week later Bob called Bill from Las Vegas after he had given the speech. "Standing O, Perkins. Standing O. I put the story of Alex at the end and brought down the house."

Bill added, "That was huge for me because in the ten years we worked together, he constantly improved that speech. And that speech may have been the best customer service speech ever given anywhere, at any time. Yet he was constantly looking for something to make it better."

But what impressed Bill the most was Bob's humility. He asked for advice to improve a great speech and then applied what he heard.

(Check out Bill's web site: BillPerkins.com)

Travis Lee was liked and respected by everyone who knew him. Travis began his career with Farrell's as a manager and was quickly promoted to General Manager of the Brea and Rancho Cucamonga stores. He was promoted to Regional Manager of those two locations, as well as Buena Park. Mike Fleming, who worked closely with Travis, told me that Parlour Enterprises and Farrell's staff appreciated his direction and leadership. Mike said, "When Marcus Lemonis became majority owner of the brand after Paul Kramer and I left the company, Travis was selected to work on the changes to Farrell's that Marcus directed. When the new Farrell's concept didn't materialize, Travis left Farrell's and formed a new company not related to the restaurant business." Travis passed away in 2023 and is survived by his wife and daughter. "His fingerprint on Farrell's will always be remembered," added Fleming.

Travis holds the trophy won by Team Farrell's at a charity event put on by Southwest Airlines, called the "Airplane Pull." Companies, including Farrell's brought a team to pull a Southwest jet across the finish line the fastest.

Travis Lee, left, and Mike Fleming pose in front of the Farrell's booth at a St. Margaret Mary Church fundraiser in Chino, California.

Travis and Mike pose with the "Richter Trophy" at the NASCAR Auto Club 400 race.

Shauna Parisi, Mike Fleming, and Travis Lee share a lighter moment at a family viewing party held at Cruiser's Bar & Grill in Newport Beach, California. Their families watched the first episode of Farrell's on *"The Profit"* television program.

Farrell's published a quarterly newsletter called "The Farrell's Sundae Funnies." The publication was distributed from 1970 through 1974. This article is from the fall 1971 edition and features the Ortman Family. Shown below, from left, Cindy, Marty, Ann "Mom," John "Pop" and President, Bruce, Laurie, and Tom Ortman. (Courtesy of Roger Baker.)

SAN DIEGO FARRELL'S IN 'FAMILY WAY'

In a sense, Farrell's San Diego is a "Mom and Pop" operation. The entire Ortman family, all seven of 'em, participate.

Headed by John C. (Pop) Ortman, who has title of president, his able assistants include Ann (Mom) as head bookkeeper; Tom, 21, manager of the Point Loma store; Cindy, 20, cashier at La Mesa; Laurie, 19, cashier and waitress at Point Loma; Marty, 14, dishwasher at Point Loma, and Bruce, 11, office maintenance manager.

John started his ice cream career as a soda jerk in his dad's drug store in St. Paul, Minn. at the age of 12, at 10c an hour. He quit at age 17 to enlist in the Navy, at $50 a month. Twenty one years later, he retired as a Lieutenant.

Following his retirement, Pop Ortman operated a fast-food drive-in in Portland until he became fascinated by Farrell's and its memories of his early "scooping" days. That was how John brought Farrell's to San Diego and Imperial counties.

FARRELL'S Family Affair, from left, Cindy, Marty, Ann, John, Bruce, Laurie and Tom Ortman.

Farrell's Restaurants Across America

Two different lists of restaurant locations appear here, and on the next two pages. The list below, courtesy of Roger Baker, shows the original locations, both company-owned and franchised. From the original stores in Portland, Oregon and northern California, Farrell's would expand via franchising. Ken McCarthy, who co-founded Farrell's with Bob Farrell, retired in 1970. (Ken McCarthy's obituary, and Wikipedia.)

This 1968 flyer, below, is courtesy of Tom Ortman, from his father, John's collection. Both Ortman's successfully ran Farrell's locations. John Ortman's 2017 obituary noted, "Farrell's was an icon in San Diego and John Ortman was a legend in the restaurant industry. He was the most successful franchisee and operated his stores longer than any other owner. His success was due to his passion for bringing a clean, wholesome family restaurant business to San Diego and being involved daily in the business."

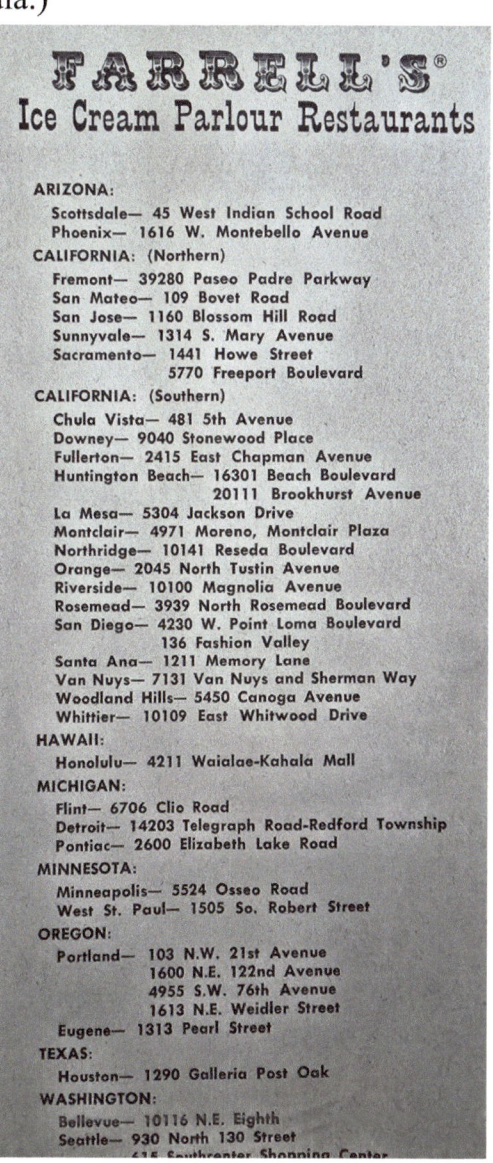

Internal Location Name	Address 1	Address 2	City, State, Zip	State
F-55: Birmingham	615 Brookwood Village		Birmingham, AL	AL
Little Rock			Little Rock, AR	AR
North Little Rock	McCain Mall	3929 McCain Blvd	North Little Rock, AR	AR
Chris-Town	Chris-Town Shopping Center	1616 W. Montebello Ave	Phoenix, AZ	AZ
Metro Pky	9647 Metro Pky W		Phoenix, AZ	AZ
Scottsdale	7145 E Indian School Rd		Scottsdale, AZ	AZ
Tempe	1301 E. Broadway Rd		Tempe, AZ	AZ
Tucson	3501 E. Broadway		Tucson, AZ	AZ
Vancouver	159 Lougheed Mall		Burnaby, British Columbia	BC
G74: Cerritos	410 Los Cerritos Ctr		Cerritos, CA	CA
Chula Vista	481 5th Ave		Chula Vista, CA	CA
F-35: Citrus Heights	5911 Sunrise Blvd		Citrus Heights, CA	CA
F-27: Daly City	138 Serramonte Center		Daly City, CA	CA
G-61: Downey	Stonewood Shopping Center		Downey, CA	CA
El Cajon	287 Fletcher Pky		El Cajon, CA	CA
Escondido	1205 E Valley Pky		Escondido, CA	CA
F-22: Fremont	39280 Paseo Padre Pky		Fremont, CA	CA
F-33: Fresno	5126 N. Palm Ave		Fresno, CA	CA
G-64: Fullerton	2415 E. Chapman Ave		Fullerton, CA	CA
F-26: Hayward	500 Southland Mall		Hayward, CA	CA
G-67: Huntington Beach	16301 Beach Blvd		Huntington Beach, CA	CA
G-71: Brookhurst	Two Guys Shopping Center	20111 Brookhurst St	Huntington Beach, CA	CA
La Jolla	La Jolla Drive		La Jolla, CA	CA
La Mesa	5304 Jackson Dr		La Mesa, CA	CA
G-62: Montclair	4971 Moreno - Montclair Plaza		Montclair, CA	CA
G-68: Northridge	10141 Rededa Blvd		Northridge, CA	CA
G-72: Orange	2045 N. Tustin St		Orange, CA	CA
G-70: Riverside	10100 Magnolia Ave		Riverside, CA	CA
G-69: Rosemead	3939 Rosemead Blvd		Rosemead, CA	CA
F-31: Howe Avenue	1441 Howe Ave		Sacramento, CA	CA
F-32: Crossroads	Freeport Blvd		Sacramento, CA	CA
F-34: Sacramento-Downtown Plaza	Downtown Plaza	547 L St	Sacramento, CA	CA
Fashion Valley	Fashion Valley Mall		San Diego, CA	CA
Point Loma	4230 W. Point Loma Blvd		San Diego, CA	CA
F-24: Blossom Hill	1330 Blossom Hill Rd		San Jose, CA	CA
F-25: Eastridge	398 Eastridge Mall		San Jose, CA	CA
F-21: San Mateo	109 Bovet Rd		San Mateo, CA	CA
G-65: Santa Ana	1211 W Memory Ln		Santa Ana, CA	CA
F-23: Sunnyvale	1314 S Mary Ave		Sunnyvale, CA	CA
G-73: Torrance	23705 Hawthorne Blvd		Torrance, CA	CA
G-66: Van Nuys	7131 Van Nuys Blvd		Van Nuys, CA	CA
G-63: Whittier	10109 Whittwood Dr		Whittier, CA	CA
G-60: Woodland Hills	5450 Canoga Ave		Woodland Hills, CA	CA
Denver	Cinderella City Shopping Cer	701 W. Hampden Ave	Englewood, CO	CO
Northglenn	Northglenn Mall	10590 Melody Dr	Northglenn, CO	CO
F-53: Altamonte Springs	451 Altamonte Dr		Altamonte Springs, FL 32701	FL
F-51: Hialeah	Westland Mall	1645 W 49th St	Hialeah, FL 33012	FL
F-52: St. Petersburg	Tyrone Square Shopping Ctr	6901 22nd Ave N	St. Petersburg, FL	FL
F-56: Tampa	2200 E Fowler Ave		Tampa, FL	FL
G-43: West Shore	341 West Shore Plaza		Tampa, FL 33609	FL
Piedmont Rd	3330 Piedmont Rd NE		Atlanta, GA	GA
Cumberland	1109 Cumberland Mall		Atlanta, GA 30339	GA
Northlake	1169 Northlake Mall		Atlanta, GA 30345	GA
Macon	Macon Mall	3661 Eisenhower Pkwy	Macon, GA	GA
Pearl Ridge	98 Moanalua Rd		Aiea, HI	HI
Kahala	Kahala Mall	4211 Waialea Ave	Honolulu, HI	HI
Ala Moana	Ala Moana Center		Honolulu, HI 96814	HI
Int'l Market Place	International Market Place	230 Kalakaua	Honolulu, HI 96815	HI
Royal Hawaiian	Royal Hawaiian Center		Honolulu, HI 96815	HI
Kaneohe	46 Kamahameha Hwy		Kaneohe, HI	HI
Maui	Maui Mall, Kahului		Maui, HI 96732	HI
Market Place at Coconut Plantation	Market Place at Coconut Plantation,		Waipouli, Kauai	HI
G-28: Ford City	Ford City Shopping Center	7451S. Cicero Ave	Chicago, IL	IL
G-29: North Riverside	North Riverside Shopping Ctr		North Riverside, IL	IL
F-68: Peoria	126 Northwoods Mall		Peoria, IL	IL
F-63: Schaumburg	Woodfield Mall		Schaumburg, IL	IL
F-65: Castleton Square	Castleton Square Shopping (	6020 E. 82nd St	Indianapolis, IN	IN
F-72: Washington St.	Washington Square Shopping Ctr		Indianapolis, IN	IN
F-67: South Bend	1421 Scottsdale Mall		South Bend, IN	IN
F-79: Wichita	1014 Towne East Square		Wichita, KS 67207	KS
G-41: Louisville	Oxmoor Shopping Ctr	7900 Shelbyville Rd	Louisville, KY	KY
F-48: New Orleans	The Plaza Shopping Center	5700 Read Blvd	New Orleans, LA 70127	LA
G-12: Baltimore	Golden Ring Mall	8642 Pulaski Hwy	Baltimore, MD	MD
G-08: Bethesda	5460 Westbard Ave		Bethesda, MD	MD
G-01: Landover	2401 Brightseat Rd		Hyattsville, MD	MD
G-03: Wheaton	Wheaton Plaza	11160 Viers Mill Rd	Wheaton, MD	MD
G-36: Ann Arbor	Briarwood Mall	470 Briarwood Circle	Ann Arbor, MI 48014	MI
G-32: Redford	Bavarian Village	14203 Telegraph Rd	Detroit, MI	MI
G-31: Flint			Flint, MI	MI
G-34: Grand Rapids	3323 28th St SE		Grand Rapids, MI	MI
G-30: Pontiac			Pontiac, MI	MI
G-33: Southfield	29285 Southfield Rd		Southfield, MI	MI
G-35: Troy	Oakland Mall	402 W 14th St	Troy, MI 48084	MI
Maplewood	1146 Maplewood Mall		Maplewood, MN	MN

Brookdale	5524 Brooklyn Blvd		Minneapolis, MN	MN
Minnneapolis	9830 Aldrich Ave S.		Minneapolis, MN	MN
Har-Mar	Snelling Ave & Country Rd B		Roseville, MN	MN
West St. Paul	1505 S. Robert St		St Paul, MN	MN
Charlotte	5413 Eastland Mall, Central Ave		Charlotte, NC 28212	NC
Fayetteville	302 Cross Creek Mall		Fayetteville, NC 28301	NC
G-20: Deptford	Deptford Mall	Clements Bridge Rd & Almonesson Rd	Deptford, NJ 08096	NJ
G-10: East Brunswick	Brunswick Square Shopping	Rte 18 & Rues Ln, Room 540	East Brunswick, NJ 08816	NJ
G-09: Paramus	624 Paramus Park		Paramus, NJ 07652	NJ
Albuquerque	203 Winrock		Albuquerque, NM 87110	NM
Massapequa			Massapequa, NY	NY
G-06: Staten Island	133A Staten Island Mall	2655 Richmond Ave	Staten Island, NY 10314	NY
F-75: Springdale	Casinelli Square Shopping Ctr		Cincinnatti, OH	OH
F-66: Columbus	Graceland Shopping Center	30 Graceland Blvd	Columbus, OH 43214	OH
F-62: Toledo	154 Franklin Park Mall		Toledo, OH 43263	OH
Oklahoma City	Crossroads Mall	7000 Crossroads Mall	Oklahoma City, OK 73149	OK
Eugene	1313 Pearl St		Eugene, OR	OR
F-11: Burnside	2100 W Burnside St		Portland, OR	OR
F-13: Lloyd Center	1613 NE Weidler St		Portland, OR	OR
F-14: 122nd & Halsey	1600 NE 122nd Ave		Portland, OR	OR
F-17: Washington Square	Washington Square Shoppin	9730 SW Washington Sq. Rd	Portland, OR	OR
F-12: Raleigh Hills	4955 SW 76th St		Raleigh Hills, OR	OR
Salem	2605 Commercial St SE		Salem, OR	OR
G-07: Langhorne	14 Oxford Valley Mall	2300 E. Old Lincoln Hwy	Langhorne, PA 19047	PA
G-11: Media	Granite Run Mall	1067 W Baltimore Pike, #211	Media, PA 19063	PA
F-47: Beaumont	304 Parkdale Mall		Beaumont, TX 77706	TX
F-46: Valley View	2118 Valley View Center		Dallas, TX	TX
El Paso	Cielo Vista Mall	8600 Gateway Blvd, W	El Paso, TX 79925	TX
F-41: Galleria	Galleria Shopping Center	5015 Westheimer Rd	Houston, TX	TX
F-59: Northwest Mall	564 Northwest Mall		Houston, TX	TX
F-58: Almeda	564 Almeda Mall		Houston, TX 77018	TX
F-42: Mesquite	2034 Town East Mall		Mesquite, TX	TX
Murray	6265 Fashion Place		Murray, UT 81047	UT
G02: Tysons Corner	8034 Tysons Corner Ctr		McLean, VA	VA
G15: Richmond	1404 Parham Rd		Richmond, VA	VA
G04: Springfield	6684 Springfield Plaza		Springfield, VA	VA
G51: Bellevue	10116 NE 8th St		Bellevue, WA	WA
G-54: Kennewick	N. Columbia Center Blvd		Kennewick, WA	WA
G52: 130th St Seattle	930 N 130th St		Seattle, WA	WA
G53: Southcenter	615 Southcenter Mall		Seattle, WA	WA
G56: Northgate	500 Northgate East Dr		Seattle, WA 98125	WA
G55: Tacoma	1056 Tacoma Mall		Tacoma WA 98409	WA
F-61: Greendale	Southridge Shopping Center	5300 S 76th St	Greendale, WI 53129	WI
F-64: Milwaukee	Northridge Shopping Center	7700 W. Brown Deer Rd	Milwaukee, WI	WI

The Farrell's location in Southfield, Michigan was described as a "Sweet Addition to the Suburbs." Local columnist Danny Raskin wrote on October 1, 1971, that the "Invitational Party Only Opening of Farrell's Ice Cream Parlour Restaurant in Southfield is October 10, 1971, with its opening to the public October 12." The grand opening of the Southfield Farrell's, located at 29285 Southfield Road just north of Twelve Mile, was attended by city officials and their families from Southfield, Oak Park, Beverly Hills, Lathrup Village, and Birmingham. Fred Daye and his Dixieland Band provided entertainment. Southfield Mayor Norman Feder had the honor of being the "Official Ribbon Cutter." (Photos provided by Richard I. Weiss with thanks to Jon Nachman and the Detroit Jewish News for background research and the ads below.)

The photo above is of the Southfield, Michigan Farrell's and the Farrell's Plaza parking lot and sign. Jon Nachman provided this, and other images taken during his birthday party, after the opening in 1971.

Farrell's Ice Cream Parlour on Telegraph Road, Redford, Michigan, August 1971. Standing in front of the Soda Fountain are, L to R, Craig Lincoln, Paul Baird, and unidentified friends and co-workers.

The image, at right, was taken from an ad in the back of an Oakland County, Michigan high school yearbook. Unsure of the location. (Courtesy of Dr. Chuck Domstein.)

The images above and at left are from the Brea location, May 2014, courtesy of Richard I. Weiss. The Brea postcard, upper left, was purchased in the auction by the author.

Below, attending the Grand Opening of Brea, from left, Shauna Parisi, Robbin Fleming, Bob and Mona Farrell, Mike Fleming, and Ryan Fleming. On the wall behind them is the plaque that appears below, right, dated 2012. (Courtesy of Mike Fleming.)

Several images from inside the Brea location, including the restaurant, above, the candy shop at left, and the fountain, below. (Photos provided by Doug Amaro, a partner in this Farrell's location.)

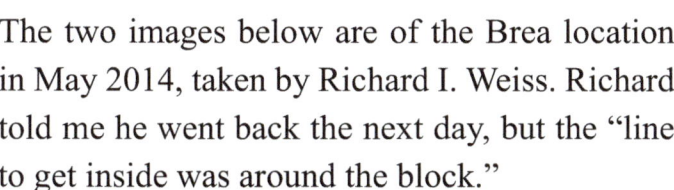

The two images below are of the Brea location in May 2014, taken by Richard I. Weiss. Richard told me he went back the next day, but the "line to get inside was around the block."

Rachel, Tina, and Nancy Legault at Farrell's Ice Cream Parlour, Briarwood Mall, Michigan.

"With nicknames like 'Triple Trouble' the Legault triplets have to be good-natured. The three (from left) Rachel, Tina, and Nancy, often confuse people at school, and make heads turn at Farrell's Ice Cream Parlour in the Briarwood Mall, too." (Courtesy of, and published by the Ann Arbor News, June 12, 1981.)

I was able to speak with two of the three young ladies about their experience working at Farrell's. They worked the same shift at the Briarwood Mall after high school. Even after they went to three different colleges, they came back to work at Farrell's in the summer. The Ann Arbor News reported that the triplets were actively involved in the school's music program, and all performed as a "trio on the synchronized swim team."

Farrell's sponsored an ice-cream eating contest at Briarwood Mall in September 1978. (Photos by Robert Chase, Ann Arbor News.)

The management and staff of Mission Viejo made it a successful location. Paul Kramer, co-owner, is standing in the back row, center, just in front of the man who is towering above everyone, under the banner. Co-owner Mike Fleming is standing, third from right. On Mike's left is the late Cathy Nail (who recently passed away). Cathy was a Regional Manager. To Cathy's left is Chad Currie, one of the managers. (Photo courtesy of Mike Fleming.)

A staff member at Mission Viejo is focused on making the perfect ice cream sundae.

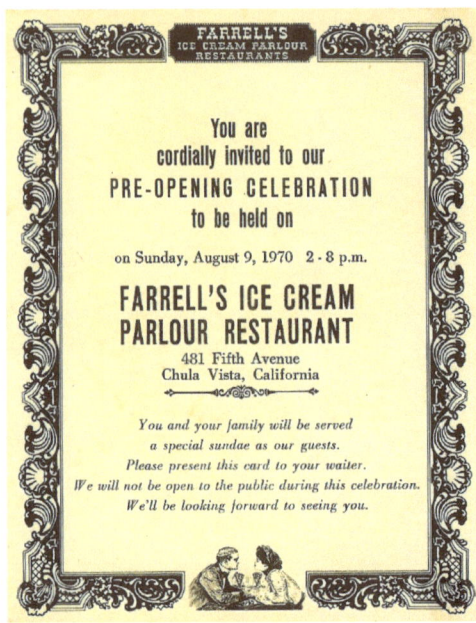

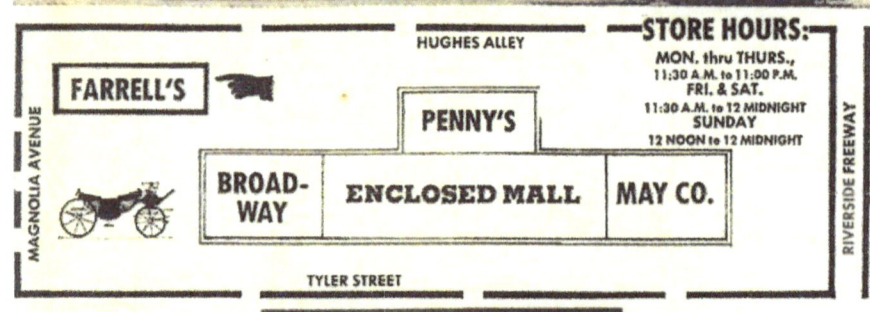

Above….

Hawaii!

Raleigh Hills, Portland Grand Opening, 1967.

Below, Brian Goodluck serves up a float to customers at Farrell's Ice Cream Parlour at El Con Mall on March 31, 1980. (Photo by Art Grasberger. Copyright Arizona Daily Star.)

Right, the Rancho Cucamonga Farrell's opened in 2011, but closed in 2016. David Allen, who authored an article in the Inland Valley Daily Bulletin noted, "It's fitting that their last day was a Sundae, I mean, Sunday." (Courtesy of Mike Fleming.)

Mike Fleming, CEO, front row left by the Statue of Liberty, with Travis Lee next to him. Travis would serve as general manager at Brea and then as Regional Manager, besides Cathy Nail. Paul Kramer, then President of Farrell's, is standing second row from the back on the left by the round light. In front of Kramer, with his hands resting on the counter, is Ron Atkinson, the general manager. With them are the rest of the team of employees and management from the Riverside, California location. Customers voiced many positive comments about the atmosphere, food, and service. Paul Kramer, then President of Farrell's Ice Cream Parlour, was interviewed at the time of the grand opening. He noted, "This is our fifth and largest Farrell's, with a large ice cream area and large candy area." Paul said, "We interviewed 1,700 people for this location, and we brought on 170 to work with us. Our cast members are absolutely fantastic." When it closed, media and customers alike, all commented that, "Closure of Farrell's Ice Cream Parlour in Riverside is really a shame." (Courtesy of Mike Fleming.)

Courtesy of John Ortman, a painting of a model Farrell's Ice Cream Parlour.

Farrell's store front, California, 1980. (Ortman collection.)

Above, from the original Portland opening, September 1963. Caught for speeding? Below, right, from the Portland location "before tearing out the walls." Below, left, the original Farrell's, Portland, Oregon, 1963. (All images courtesy of John Ortman collection.)

FARRELL'S FOUNTAIN MENU

Farrell's was known for its birthday celebrations, an atmosphere that included waitstaff in retro garb, banging drums and singing happy birthday to the celebrants and their guests. Farrell's was also known for their tasty variety of meticulously made and beautifully presented, fabulous fountain favorites. The following pages include a sampling of fountain items from the later years (dated 2012), as well as the earlier fountain sundaes from the initial years. These "job aids" guided employees in building each sundae, in proper order. At the bottom of each item, it states: "If it's not a ten… Make it again."

Fountain Job Aids - Table of Contents

Item	Page	Item	Page
Gold Digger	2	ZOO	24
Parlour's Tin Roof	3	Custom Concoctions	25
Black & White	4	Shakes	26
Oreo Bliss	5	Ice Cream Sodas	27
Mocha Nut	6	Ice Cream Floats	28
Banana Split	7	Freezes – Sherbet**	29
Banana Royal	8	Corner Favorites	30
Straw – Ana	9	Just for Kids	31
Rocky Road	10	Fake Chicken Dinner	32
Gold Rush	11	Service Ware	33
Nutty Nutty	12	Plate Presentation	34
Hot Fudge Sundae	13	Eating Challenge	35
Hot Luncheons	14	Hot Fudge Cookie**	36
Carmel Nugget	15	Any Day Sundae**	37
Triple Choc. Brownie	16	Strawberry Shortcake**	38
Nachos	17	Super Purist**	39
Brownie Eruption	18	Kathy's Hawaiian Vacation**	40
Caramel Apple Blossom	19		
Pig's Trough	20		
Gibson Girl	21		
Mt Saint Helen	22		
Volcano	23		

** = not on current Menu

Whip Cream: 15 ounces of heavy whipping cream plus 1 ounce of vanilla syrup in a one-liter isi dispenser.

 * Fill multiple dispensers by using a 60 ounce pitcher of cream and 5 pumps (5 oz) of vanilla syrup.

Hot Topping: 130° **1 Pump = 1 ounce**

Finished Weight: Place an empty dish on scale and zero the weight. Sundaes contents are measured before whip cream, final nuts or cherry.

Read all job aids and ice cream portions before starting.

The data in this document incorporates proprietary rights of Farrell's. Any party accepting this document does so in confidence & agrees that it shall not be duplicated nor disclosed without consent. Copyright ©2011 Farrell's & Parlour Enterprises, Inc.

6/16/2012

The Pig's Trough

Weight: 25.5 oz
Before whip cream, nuts & cherry

READ AND BUILD FROM BOTTOM UP

Dish: Pig Dish and Two Farrell's Flags
Garnish: Wooden Trough Holder

Ingredients	Portions	Directions
Cherry w/stem	3 each	Place on top of each crown of whip cream.
Almonds, chopped	3 tsp.	Sprinkle over whipped cream.
Whipped Cream	3 - 3 oz crowns	Place a crown of whip cream on center-top of each set of ice cream scoops
Banana	2 each	Cut banana in half-lengthwise and place one-half on each side of ice cream (cut side facing ice cream).
Pineapple Topping	2 oz	Place over chocolate ice cream.
Chocolate Topping	2 oz	Pump over strawberry ice cream.
Strawberry Topping	2 oz	Place over vanilla ice cream.
Chocolate Ice Cream	2 – (4 oz scoop)	Scoop into dish, place next to strawberry ice cream.
Strawberry Ice Cream	2 – (4 oz scoop)	Scoop into dish, place next to vanilla ice cream.
Vanilla Ice Cream	2 – (4 oz scoop)	Scoop into dish.

Dish: Pig Dish

Standard Service Time: 7 minutes
Section Code: Belly Busters
© Farrell's 2006

If it's not a ten — Make it again.

The Zoo

Weight: 5.5 lbs ice cream

READ AND BUILD FROM BOTTOM UP

Dish: Zoo Bowl
Garnish: 4 Chenille Animal Picks, 4 Plastic Animal Picks = 8 total.

Ingredients	Portions	Directions
Banana halves cherry / US flag	6 each	Cut three bananas in half and place US flag / through a cherry on the flat side of cut banana. Place these standing up, around the outer rim of bowl.
Whipped Cream	6 - 3 oz crowns	Place whipped cream in center area
Raspberry Syrup	3 oz	Place on top of ice cream
Chocolate Syrup	3 oz, 3 ladles	Place on top of ice cream
Strawberry Topping	3 oz, 3 ladles	Place on top of ice cream
Pineapple Topping	3 oz, 3 ladles	Place on top of ice cream
Vanilla Ice Cream	1 – 8oz slab	Place slabs in bottom of bowl.
Rainbow Sherbet	2 – 8oz slabs	Place slabs in bottom of bowl.
Mint Choc Chip Ice Cream	2 – 8oz slabs	Place slabs in bottom of bowl.
Strawberry Ice Cream	2 – 8oz slabs	Place slabs in bowl on top of vanilla and chocolate ice cream.
Chocolate Ice Cream	2 – 8oz slabs	Place slabs in bottom of bowl.
Vanilla Ice Cream	2 – 8oz slabs	Place slabs in bottom of bowl. Place slabs of ice cream in fanned-ou circular formation in bowl.

Standard Service Time: 10 minutes
© Farrell's 2011

Section Code: Belly Busters

If it's not a ten — FARRELL'S ICE CREAM PARLOUR RESTAURANTS — Make it again.

Securely loading The Zoo to prepare for parading around the restaurant to the table with the lucky guests!

Parlour's Tin Roof

Weight: 9.0 oz
Before whip cream, final nuts & cherry

READ AND BUILD FROM BOTTOM UP
Garnish: N/A

Ingredients	Portions	Directions
Cherry w/stem	1 each	Place on top of whip cream.
Spanish Peanuts	1 tsp.	Place on top of hot fudge and ice cream.
Whipped Cream	2 oz crown	Place on top of fudge and peanuts.
Spanish Peanuts	1 tsp.	Place on top of hot fudge and ice cream.
Hot Fudge Topping	1 oz. (1 pump)	Pump over ice cream.
Vanilla Ice Cream	2 – 4 oz scoops	Scoop an elongated scoop of ice cream into bottom of glass, then add second scoop.
Spanish Peanuts	1 tsp. (approx. 10-15 peanuts)	Drop into glass.
Hot Fudge Topping	½ oz (1/2 pump)	Swirl inside glass, not on bottom.

Dish: 12 oz pedestal

Standard Service Time: 5 minutes Section Code: Sundaes
© Farrell's 2011

If it's not a ten  Make it again.

Banana Split

Weight: 16.75 oz
Before banana whip cream, nuts & cherry

READ AND BUILD FROM BOTTOM UP
Garnish: US Flag

Ingredients	Portions	Directions
Cherry w/stem	1 each	Place on top of whip cream.
Chopped Almonds	½ tsp.	Sprinkle over whipped cream.
Whipped Cream	3 crowns (2 oz each)	Place each crown on top of the ice cream pyramid.
Banana	1 each	Cut banana in half-lengthwise and place one-half On each side of ice cream (cut side facing ice cream).
Pineapple Topping	1 oz (1 ladle)	Pump over chocolate ice cream.
Chocolate Topping	1 oz (1 ladle)	Pump over strawberry ice cream.
Strawberry Topping	1 oz (1 ladle)	Pump over vanilla ice cream.
Strawberry Ice Cream	4 oz scoop	Scoop on top of vanilla and chocolate, while pressing vanilla and chocolate together, to form a pyramid.
Chocolate Ice Cream	4 oz scoop	Scoop into dish, place next to vanilla ice cream.
Vanilla Ice Cream	4 oz scoop	Scoop into dish.

Dish: Split, 11" oval plate, doily
Standard Service Time: 5 minutes
Section Code: Sundaes
© Farrell's 2011

If it's not a ten  Make it again.

Gibson Girl

Weight: 19 oz
Before whip cream, nuts & cherry

READ AND BUILD FROM BOTTOM UP
Dish: Goblet Glass
Garnish: Two Farrell's Flags

Ingredients	Portions	Directions
Cherry w/stem	1 each	Place on top of whip cream.
Almonds, chopped	1 teaspoon	Sprinkle over whipped cream
Whipped Cream	3 oz crown	Place whip on center-top of cake.
Butterscotch Topping	1 – 1 oz pump	Pump butterscotch topping into glass.
Cherry Syrup	1 – 1 oz pump	Pump cherry syrup into glass.
Rainbow Sherbet	3 (4 oz scoop)	Place all (3) three sherbets in triangle-fashion side-by-side on top of vanilla ice cream.
Vanilla Ice Cream	3 (4 oz scoops)	Place vanilla scoops into glass on top of syrups.
Butterscotch Topping	1 – 1 oz pump	Pump butterscotch topping into glass.
Cherry Syrup	1 – 1 oz pump	Pump cherry syrup into glass.

Dish: Goblet Glass

Standard Service Time: 7 minutes
Section Code: Belly Busters

If it's not a ten   FARRELL'S ICE CREAM PARLOUR RESTAURANTS   Make it again.

Mt. Saint Helen

Weight: 17.5 oz
Before whip cream, nuts & cherry

READ AND BUILD FROM BOTTOM UP
Garnish: Farrell's Flag
Garnish: One sugar cube dipped in lemon extract – light before serving.

Ingredients	Portions	Directions
Cherry w/stem	1 each	Place on top of whip cream, on side.
Whipped Cream	3 oz crown	Place cream around the scoop of strawberry ice cream.
Strawberry Ice cream	1 - 4 oz scoop	Place in center.
Almonds, chopped	1 teaspoon	Sprinkle over vanilla ice cream, near glass rim.
Hot fudge	2 pumps	Pump over vanilla ice cream.
Vanilla ice cream	2 - 4 oz scoops	Place over Carmel, between the choc scoops
Carmel, hot	2 pumps	Pump over choc. Ice cream.
Chocolate Ice Cream	3 - 4 oz scoops	Place in glass in triangle form.

Dish: Goblet Glass

Standard Service Time: 7 minutes   Section Code: Belly Busters
© Farrell's 2006

If it's not a ten   FARRELL'S ICE CREAM PARLOUR RESTAURANTS   Make it again.

Hot Fudge Volcano

Weight: 120 oz
(7 lbs, 8 ounces)
Before whip cream, nuts & cherry

READ AND BUILD FROM BOTTOM UP

Dish: Mountain Dish
Garnish: 12 oz. Pedestal Glass of Hot Fudge Farrell's Flag & Sparkler.

Ingredients	Portions	Directions
Sparkler	1	Server to light at table side during announcement. Do not carry lit flame, hold volcano until sparkler is out. Put sparkler in water after use.
Hot Fudge	11 oz (11.5oz glass)	AT TABLE: Server is to pour ¼ of the hot fudge topping over top of the volcano. Leave the rest for the guest to use.
Nuts	2 tbl. sp.	Sprinkle over volcano.
Cherries	16 each	Place cherries evenly spaced on whip cream ring.
Whipped Cream	2 oz ring	Place a ring of whipped cream around base
Vanilla Ice Cream	30 – 4 oz scoops	Scoop vanilla ice cream into a pyramid-like shape. Scooping ice cream into 7 stacked layers (each scoop should be 4 oz):

Layer 7 1 vanilla
Layer 6 3 vanilla
Layer 5 4 vanilla
Layer 4 4 vanilla
Layer 3 5 vanilla
Layer 2 6 vanilla
Layer 1 7 vanilla

Standard Service Time: 10 minutes
© Farrell's 2011

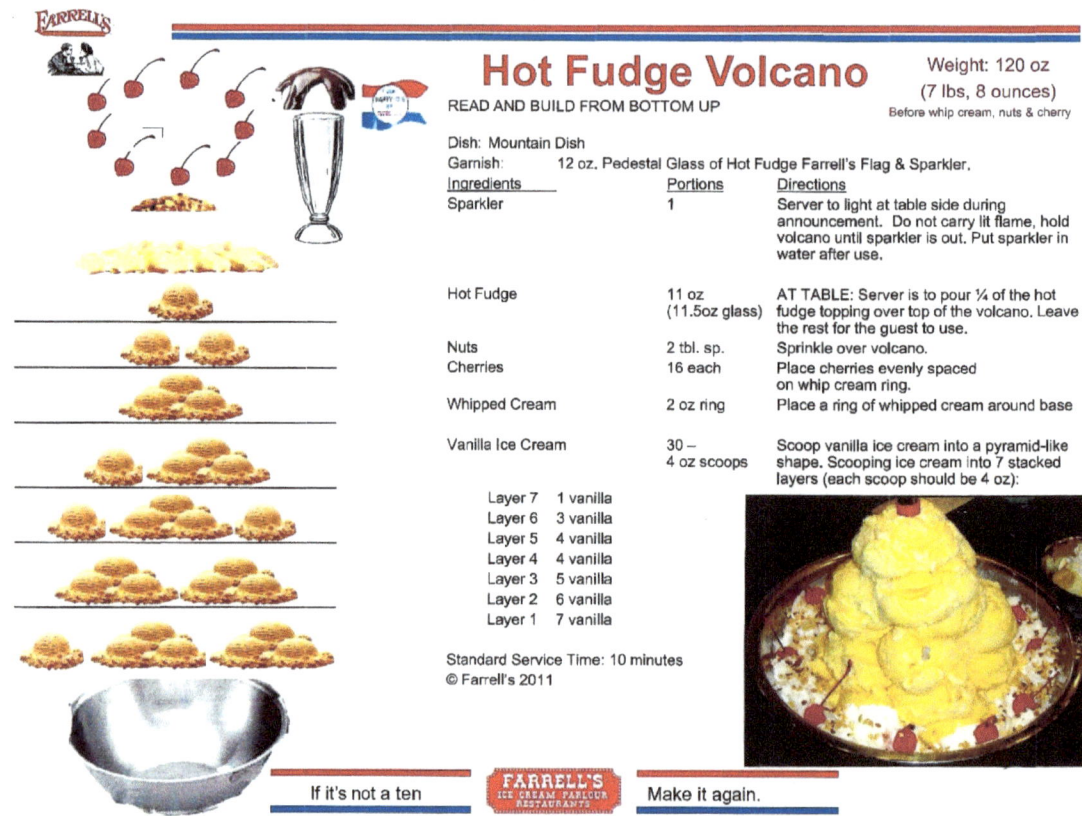

If it's not a ten — FARRELL'S ICE CREAM PARLOUR RESTAURANTS — Make it again.

Shakes

READ AND BUILD FROM BOTTOM UP

Garnish: Large straw. Served with remaining mix in clean metal shake cup.

Ingredients	Portions	Directions
Cherry w/ stem	1	Place on top of whipped cream
Chocolate Shavings	.25 ounce	Sprinkle over Whip Cream.
Whipped Cream	1 ounce	Place rosette on top.

Finish: Pour mixture into a 12-ounce pedestal glass. Pour remaining mixture into a clean metal shake cup and serve both.

Mix: first on low speed, then medium, then high. As the speed is increased the contents of the cup should not splash out. When finished, all the ice cream is to be dissolved into the mixture. The product will be solid enough that a spoon will stand in the center by itself, but liquid enough to be consumed through a straw.

Malt or Oreo Crumbles	1 ounce if ordered.	Add malt or finely crushed Oreo crumbles
Milk	approx ½ cup	Add approximately ½ cup of whole milk up to the second "dimple" on the mix cup. Approximately 3" from the top.
Flavored Syrups	2 ounces (2 pumps)	Add two ounces (one pump) of flavored syrup desired.
Vanilla Ice Cream	2 - 4 oz scoops	Scoop ice cream into metal shake cup

Glass: 12 oz. Pedestal Glass
Standard Service Time: 5 minutes
© Farrell's 2006

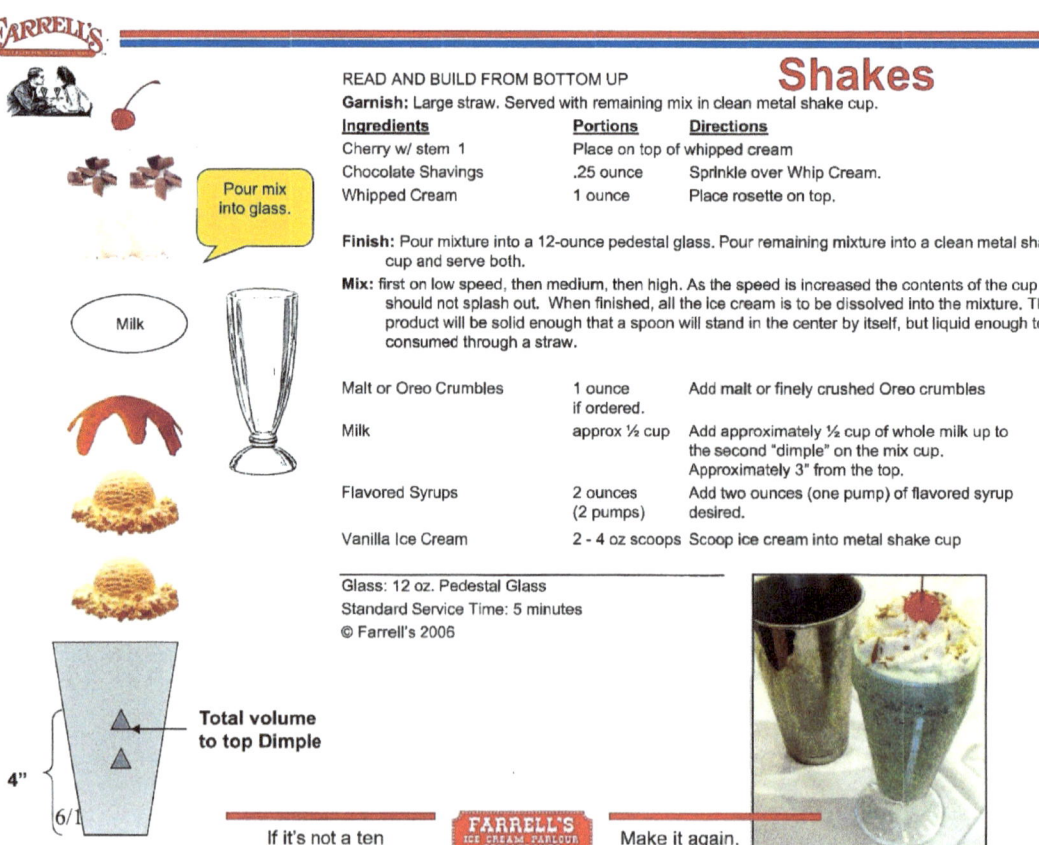

If it's not a ten — FARRELL'S ICE CREAM PARLOUR RESTAURANTS — Make it again.

Just for Kids: Sundaes & Float

READ AND BUILD FROM BOTTOM UP

Ingredients	Portions	Directions

Follow instruction for regular banana split – reduce ALL portions in half.

CLOWN SUNDAE

Ingredients	Portions	Directions
Color Sprinkles	1 tsp	Sprinkles on top of whip cream.
Cherry	1	Place cherry on front to form the nose.
Whip Cream	2; .5 ounce	Place small crowns of whip cream on sides.
Sugar Cone	1 cone	Place on side of ice cream forming hat.
Vanilla Ice Cream	4 ounce scoop	Place in dish

FLOAT

Ingredients	Portions	Directions
Cherry w/ stem	1	Place on top of whipped cream
Vanilla Ice Cream	1 – 4 ounce	Scoop portions of ice cream into cup.
Soft Drink - Pop	4 ounces	Fill the glass with pop of choice. Leave room for the ice cream.
		Cola, Diet Cola, Root Beer, Lemon Lime, or Orange.

SHAKE

Follow instructions on shake job aid. One 4 ounce scoop and one 2 ounce scoop.

Standard Service Time: 5 minutes   Section Code: Just For Kids
© Farrell's 2011

6/16/2012

 If it's not a ten   **FARRELL'S** ICE CREAM PARLOUR RESTAURANTS   Make it again.

Kathy's Hawaiian Vacation

Toasted Coconut

Toasted Coconut

Marshmallow

Pineapple - Coconut
Ice Cream

Marshmallow

READ AND BUILD FROM BOTTOM UP
Garnish: Farrell's Flag

Ingredients	Portions	Directions
Cherry w/stem	1 each	Place on top of whip cream.
Coconut, Toasted	½ tsp.	Sprinkle over whip cream.
Whipped Cream	¾ oz crown	Place on top of topping.
Coconut, Toasted	½ tsp.	Sprinkle over marshmallow.
Pineapple Topping	2 oz	
Marshmallow Topping	¾ oz. (1 pump)	Pump over ice cream.
Pineapple Coconut Ice Cream	2 (4 oz scoops)	Place inside bowl.
Marshmallow Topping	½ oz (1/2 pump)	Swirl inside bowl.

Dish: 5" Bowl

Standard Service Time: 5 minutes

If it's not a ten   **FARRELL'S** ICE CREAM PARLOUR RESTAURANTS   Make it again.

KRISTY'S DELIGHT

KRISTY DISH
#20 SCOOP

1. Scoop 2 oz. spumoni ice cream.
2. Scoop 2 oz. coffee ice cream.
3. Scoop 2 oz. vanilla ice cream.
4. Pump 1½ oz. caramel topping onto the coffee ice cream.
5. Pump 1½ oz. chocolate topping onto the vanilla ice cream.
6. Pump 1½ oz. marshmallow topping onto the spumoni ice cream.
7. Place a crown of whipped cream over the three scoops of ice cream.
8. Sprinkle nuts over the whipped cream.
9. Top with a cherry half.
10. Top also with a GIRAFFE ZOO PIK.

KATHY'S PINK SURPRISE

KATHY DISH
#20 SCOOP

1. Scoop three 2 oz. scoops vanilla ice cream into dish.
2. Pump 1½ oz. strawberry topping over ice cream.
3. Slice one banana lengthwise and also crosswise. Stand three parts upright around the edge of the dish and place the fourth part on top of the ice cream.
4. Place a crown of whipped cream over the three scoops of ice cream.
5. Sprinkle nuts over the whipped cream.
6. Top with a cherry half.
7. Top also with a PINK ELEPHANT ZOO PIK.

"Kristy's Delight" and "Kathy's Pink Surprise", above, and "Colleen's Salute" on the next page were named for Bob and Ramona's three daughters. A website Menu History noted that Kathy's and Colleen's sundaes would be off the menu for several years but return in 1977.

COLLEEN'S SALUTE

COLLEEN DISH
#20 SCOOP
___

1. Scoop 2 oz. vanilla ice cream.
2. Scoop 2 oz. chocolate ice cream.
3. Scoop 2 oz. strawberry ice cream.
4. Pump 1½ oz. strawberry topping onto the chocolate ice cream.
5. Pump 1½ oz. pineapple topping onto the strawberry ice cream.
6. Pump 1½ oz. blackberry topping onto the vanilla ice cream.
7. Place a crown of whipped cream over the two scoops of ice cream.
8. Sprinkle nuts over the whipped cream.
9. Top with a cherry half.
10. Top also with an AMERICAN FLAG.

CLOWN SUNDAE

CLOWN DISH
#20 SCOOP
___

1. Dip one 2 oz. scoop vanilla into dish.
2. Top with 1 oz. chocolate or strawberry topping.
3. Place a cone on top to one side.
4. Place two "ears" of whip cream, opposite each other, beside the scoop.
5. Top with half cherry and dust face with sprinkles.

BANANA ROYAL

SPLIT DISH
#20 SCOOP

1. Scoop two 2 oz. scoops vanilla ice cream side by side.
2. Pump 1½ oz. hot fudge onto each scoop of ice cream.
3. Place a ribbon of whipped cream from each end to the center.
4. Sprinkle with nuts.
5. Top with a half cherry.
6. Cut a banana lengthwise and place one half on each side of dish.

MT. HOOD BOWL
SPADE

1. Spade (5 oz.) one slice of the following flavors of ice cream, on edge, into the bowl forming a mountain:

    Vanilla, Chocolate, Butter Pecan, Strawberry, Coffee.

2. Pump 4½ oz. hot fudge topping over the top of the mountain.
3. Pump 4½ oz. hot marshmallow topping onto the hot fudge topping to create a glacier effect.
4. Place a ring of whipped cream around the base of the mountain.
5. Break two bananas into 2" chunks and place around dish in the whipped cream.
6. Pump 3 oz. strawberry topping onto the whipped cream and bananas.
7. Scatter nuts over mountain.
8. Place a flag on top of mountain.

> These three pages include early menu sundaes from the 1960s. Included are "Mt Hood," above which would be renamed "Pike's Peak." The "Portland Zoo," below, became "The Zoo." Two for the Road (not shown) would become the "Pig's Trough."

TWO ON A BLANKET

TROUGH DISH
#20 SCOOP

1. Place two slices of Pound Cake (3" x 3" x ½" thick) side by side in bottom of dish.
2. Scoop a 5 oz. scoop of chocolate ice cream and place it in the middle of a piece of pound cake.
3. Scoop a 5 oz. scoop of vanilla ice cream and place it in the middle of a piece of pound cake.
4. Pump 3 oz. of hot fudge onto the vanilla ice cream.
5. Pump 3 oz. of hot marshmallow onto the chocolate ice cream.
6. Place a strip of whipped cream around the edge of the dish and between the two scoops of ice cream.
7. Sprinkle nuts over the ice cream.
8. Top each ice cream scoop with a cherry half.

PORTLAND ZOO

ZOO BOWL
SPADE

1. Spade (5 oz.) one slice of each flavor of ice cream from all cabinets into zoo bowl. Stack one flavor on top of the other, creating a stack of ice cream in middle of bowl.
2. Spade (5 oz.) one slice of each sherbet flavor on edge around bottom of bowl.
3. Into milk shake beaker pump 3 oz. of each topping and pour over ice cream.
4. Make a ring of whipped cream around edge of bowl on top of sherbet.
5. Cut three bananas crosswise and stand the six pieces around the bowl in the whipped cream.
6. Make a rosette of whipped cream on top of each banana and top the rosette with a plastic animal.
7. Sprinkle dish with nuts and cherries.

History of the Farrell's Menus

6

Beginning with the first restaurant in 1963, the Farrell's menu opened to a simple 15.5" by 22.5" tabloid-style newspaper. The menus would evolve through the years as the kitchen food and fountain items changed and expanded. As the years went by and new stores were opened, some menus were designed especially for those locations. Promotional menus were also utilized to bring attention to specific food items and desserts. The menu included stories, history, and highlighted special treats and events. It featured appetizers, sandwiches, burgers, and dozens of different sundaes, as well as malts, shakes, sodas, and floats. Unusual offerings included a glass of soda water for two cents, and the traditional free sundae for customers celebrating a birthday. Some of the sundaes were large enough for a group to share. The largest, "The Zoo" sundae, was delivered with great fanfare by employees carrying it wildly around the restaurant on a stretcher, accompanied by the sound of ambulance sirens. (In part from Roger Baker and Wikipedia.)

The **Original Farrell's**, Portland, Oregon. This image was provided by both Tom Ortman and Dwight Manley, with appreciation.

Bob Farrell developed the kitchen items while Ken McCarthy crafted and priced the fountain items. Besides featuring waffles and egg dishes (an unusual offering considering the kitchen didn't open until 11 am), the menu also had the unique offerings on the next page.

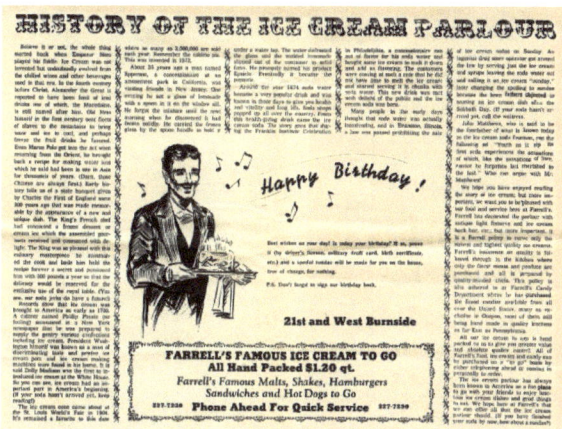

This early menu above, both front and back, was printed when only the original parlour on Burnside Road existed. The menu was a large 15.5" by 22.5".

FARRELL'S KITCHEN MENU

SANDWICHES
Served on Rye Bread with a Dill Pickle and a Side of Sauerkraut

1. Hot Corned Beef .... .85
2. Hot Pastrami .... .85
3. Hot Baked Ham .... .85
4. Hot Beef .... .85
5. Turkey .... .80
6. Swiss Cheese with Ham, Pastrami or Corned Beef ...1.20
7. Grilled Corned Beef, Sauerkraut, and Swiss Cheese (ala Reuben) 1.50

CLUB SANDWICHES
1. Turkey — Bacon — Tomato 1.25
2. Tuna — Sliced Egg — Tomato 1.15
3. Ham — Swiss Cheese — Tomato 1.50

REGULAR SANDWICHES
1. Tuna Salad .... .55
2. Turkey Salad .... .65
3. Bacon, Lettuce and Tomato .... .75
4. Grilled Cheese .... .50
5. Grilled Ham and Cheese .... .70
6. Egg Salad .... .50
7. Cream Cheese and Jelly .... .50
8. Peanut Butter and Jelly .... .50
9. Cold Meats — Corned Beef, Pastrami or Ham .... .65
10. Swiss Cheese .... .60
11. Cream Cheese and Date Nut Bread (Try this!) .... .70
12. Avocado and Bacon (When available) .... .75

KIDDIES MENU
10 AND UNDER

Egg Salad Samich	.35
Peanut Butter Samich	.30
Ham Samich	.35
Jelly Samich	.25
Cheese Samich	.35

BABY BOTTLES WARMED
And Any Special Food We Can Prepare for Your Youngster Please Ask

WAFFLES
Order by number—Our help can't read too well
Farrell's Famous Waffle Combinations—made with fresh ranch eggs and Western flour.

1. Served with syrup and butter .... .50
2. Your Choice of Ice Cream (Spaded on) .... .75
3. Grilled Ham, Bacon, Sausage .... .85
4. Bacon or Ham and Eggs 1.25
5. Melted Cheese and Bacon .... .95
6. Sliced Bananas and Hot Fudge .... .90
7. Crushed Pineapple .... .75
8. Apple Butter and Sausage .... .85
9. Melted Butter and Cinnamon Sugar .... .65
10. Apple Sauce and Bacon .... .95
11. Fruit Salad and Whipped Cream .... .90
12. Strawberries .... .90
13. Blackberries .... .80
14. Marshmallow, Hot Fudge, Almonds .... .90
15. Cottage Cheese (Old Fashioned) and Sliced Pineapple .... .90
16. Cream Cheese and Almonds .... .90
17. Two Fresh Ranch Eggs as you like 'em .... .85
18. Almonds in Syrup .... .70
*19. Choice of Ice Cream, Hot Fudge, Almonds, Sliced Bananas and Whipped Cream 1.00

*Farrell's Favorite—If you have a special concoction of waffles, let us try and make it for you. Priced accordingly.

RANCH EGGS
All fresh daily from local farms

1. Two eggs as you like 'em .... .70
2. With Sausage, Bacon or Ham .... .95
3. Scrambled Eggs with Chopped-up Ham, Corned Beef or Pastrami .... .85

Served with French Fried Potatoes and Toast
English Muffin — 10c extra
Orange Juice or Tomato Juice .... .20
Served Only 7 A.M. - 11 A.M. 7 P.M. - Closing

FRENCH TOAST COMBINATIONS
1. French Toast with Strawberries or Blackberries .... .95
2. French Toast with Two Eggs (As you like 'em) 1.10
3. French Toast with Ham, Bacon or Sausage 1.15
4. French Toast with Butter, Syrup, Honey or Jelly .... .80
Served 7 A.M. - 11 A.M. and 7 P.M. Till Closing

BEVERAGES

Coffee	.10	Sanka	.15
Tea	.15	Iced Tea & Coffee	.20
Milk	.15	Chocolate Milk	.20

Farrell's Special Hot Chocolate covered with Whipped Cream served in a Turkish Cup .... .35

HAMBURGERS
Fresh, pure ground beef prepared daily—
Served with garnish and a dill pickle
(¼ Lb. Naturally)

1. Burger with Melted Cheese and Bacon .... .80
2. Burger with Regular Garnish .... .60
3. Burger with Melted Cheese, Tomato, Grilled Onion .... .75
4. Burger with Garnish, Cheese, Bacon, Tomato, and Fries 1.00

FARRELL'S FAMOUS NEW YORK HOT DOG COMBINATION
All beef frankfurters with special seasoning—
All served on our special bun

1. Hot Dog with cold German Sauerkraut .... .55
2. Hot Dog with Mustard and Relish, or Plain .... .45
3. Hot Dog with Melted Cheddar Cheese .... .60
4. Hot Dog with Chopped Lettuce, Tomato, Onion Mayonnaise, Mustard and Special Spices .... .65
(Really Good)

HOT PLATES
Served with French Fries and Tossed Salad and Bread and Butter and Coffee or Tea

Hamburger Steak	1.50
Jumbo Butterfly Shrimp	1.70
Fish and Chips	1.50

SALADS
Your choice of Thousands, French or Roquefort Dressing

1. Chef's Fresh Vegetable Salad with Strips of Ham and Cheese 1.20
2. Old Fashioned Cottage Cheese and Fru't Salad 1.20
3. Fruit Salad—Loads of Fruit in Season Topped with Sherbet or Cottage Cheese and Whipped Cream 1.50
4. Tuna Fish Salad 1.20
5. Turkey Salad 1.20
6. Alaskan Crab Louis 2.50

All the above salads are served with melba toast and crackers
Dinner sizes of the above are half price.

FARRELL'S SIDE ORDERS AND SNACKS

Toasted Bagel with Cream Cheese—Lox—Sliced Onion—Tomato	1.50
Toasted Bagel with Cream Cheese, Lettuce and Tomato	.80
Toasted English Muffin and Jelly	.25
Lettuce Wedge	.40
Side of Cottage Cheese	.45
Cup of Soup (Of the Day)	.25
Assorted Cold Cuts, Sliced Tomatoes, Bread and Cheese	1.50
French Fries	.25
Toasted Bread and Butter	.20

DESSERTS
Check our fountain menu above for our delicious ice cream dishes

Cake	.30	Pie a la mode	.40
Cake a la mode	.40	Cheesecake (A. Farrell Special)	.50
Pound cake	.40		
Pie	.30	(With Strawberries)	.80

Table Service 25c Per Person Min.
11 A.M. - 2 P.M.   5 P.M. - 7 P.M.

This first menu is from 1962 at the 21st and West Burnside location. Courtesy of John Guest, Christophers, Inc.

Unusual food offerings included Cream Cheese on Date Nut Bread, and Avocado and Bacon Sandwich.

The Farrell's Special would be added to the menu in 1963. It was the predecessor to the gastronomicaldelicatessenepicurean's delight, which would not be featured by name for at least three more years.

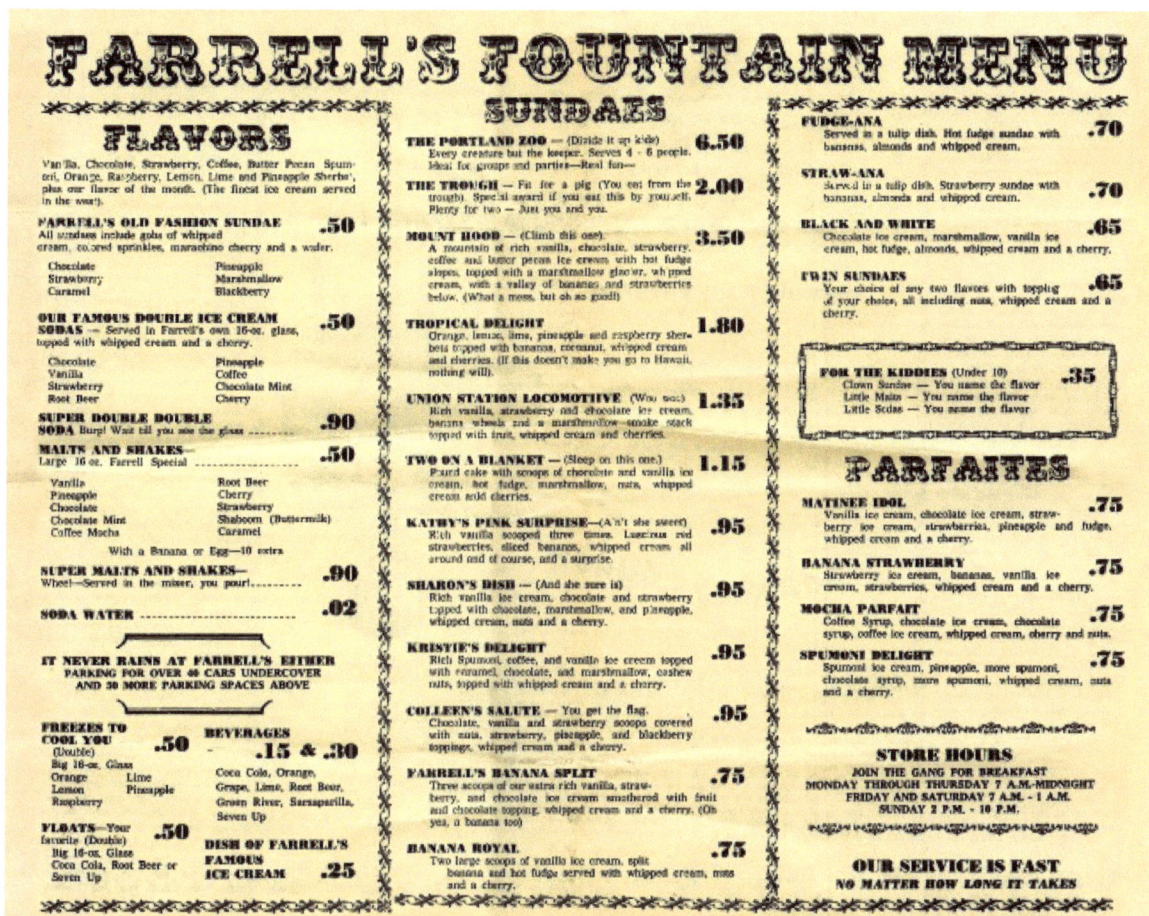

This 1962 menu had unique offerings.

Bob and Mona's daughters, Kathy, Colleen, and Kristie are highlighted! As is Ken McCarthy's daughter, Sharon.

Price of a banana split was 75 cents!

Union Station Locomotive - Woo woo - An ice cream sundae shaped into a train, using banana wheels and marshmallow smokestack. **The Zoo** was originally called the **Portland Zoo**, while the **Pike's Peak** sundae was called **Mount Hood**.

1966 - Similar in size and layout to the 1962/63 menu, this menu was printed when only four parlours were in existence: Portland-Burnside Rd, Portland-Halsey Avenue, Salem, Oregon, and Bellevue, Washington. The menu also had unique offerings:

McCarthy's Favorite - a tribute to Ken, the "other" founder of Farrell's, this lunch/dinner item consisted of scrambled eggs with corned beef, served with an English muffin and French fries.

Mother Farrell's Famous Irish Clam Chowder.

The Gibson Girl was added to the menu and featured vanilla ice cream, sherbets, grenadine and banana syrup.

The Zoo sundae was called the Woodland Park Zoo, and the Pike's Peak was called Mount Rainier.

Price of a Banana Split: $0.85

Notice the lack of the word "Restaurants" on the logo - the menus from 1963 until late 1966 featured this logo. The word "Restaurants" was added in 1966, and the resulting logo and picture was copyrighted that year. Notice the front of the 1970 menu, below with "Restaurants".

1970 The front of the menu, at left.

Territorial franchisees printed their own "flavor" of menus. This allowed them to add a local flavor and list their own parlour locations on the menu. This gem is from the Los Angeles franchise - the largest franchisee, with 12 parlours open and two more on the way. The menu was somewhat smaller than the 1963-1966 variant (13 inches wide by 10 1/2 inches high). This is Roger Baker's personal favorite, with blue text accented with red and red/blue titles.

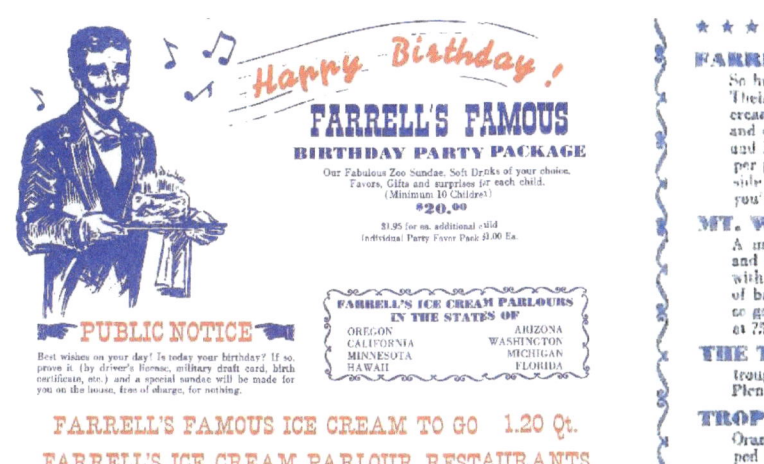

1970 - The Pike's Peak sundae was called Mt. Whitney in Los Angeles. Spumoni ice cream, pineapple sherbet, and lemon sherbet were still on the menu, but not for long. The price of a banana split: $1.09. The Trough was $2.00.

KITCHEN MENU

WE BELIEVE IN AMERICA — *WE BELIEVE IN AMERICA*

HOT DOGS

Famous New York Style — ¼-lb Frank on Our Own
Special Bun — With Garnish Tray

1. **SERVED WITH SIDE OF KRAUT** 65
2. **SERVED WITH MELTED CHEESE** 75
   With Kraut
3. **CHILI HOT DOG** (Coney Style) 95
   With Side of Chopped Onions

Perhaps the most famous hot dogs in the world (next to Nero's palace poodles) were those eaten by King George VI and Queen Elizabeth, when President Roosevelt hosted a "typical American picnic," the guests came back for seconds.... Seconds? FARRELL'S guests get Royal Treatment along with the fattest, juiciest, tastiest hot dogs in town. People really come back *for ours!* Our champ (the frankfurter supreme) is the ¼-lb. New York variety served gloriously enclosed in a Famous FARRELL'S Bun. You like sauerkraut with your Hot Dog, we provide it.

KIDDIES MENU

10 AND UNDER
(Also 65 and over)

KIDDIE HANGERBER 65
CHEESE SAMICH 35
**PEANUT BUTTER
& JELLY SAMICH** 35
CLOWN SUNDAE 35
Chocolate or Strawberry Topping
LITTLE SHAKES 35
Chocolate or Strawberry
LITTLE SODAS 35
Chocolate or Strawberry

BABY BOTTLES WARMED
And Any Special Food We Can Prepare for Your
Youngster Please Ask

15¢ Extra for Grilled Sandwiches

SIDE ORDERS

TOSSED GREEN SALAD 40
Served with your favorite dressing
SIDE OF FRENCH FRIES 30
(Shoestring style)
OUR FAMOUS CHILI
(Cooked slowly with lean meat and plump red beans)
Cup .40   Large Bowl 75
YOUR OWN BIRTHDAY CAKE
cut and served 1.00

HAMBURGERS

Fresh Pure Ground Beef Prepared Daily — Served With Garnish Tray
Our Own Special Onion Roll Bun

Salisbury steak owes its name to a food-faddist-physician who urged a thrice daily diet of ground beefsteak (no buns) for relief from many human ills. (The diet didn't do much for beef cattle; they think he gave people a bum steer.) FARRELL'S Hamburgers, however, are *something else*: flavorful, tantalizing, tender beef, happily cradled in the most succulent of delicacies, that baker's dream of bunney (FANFARE!) FARRELL'S Famous Onion Roll Bun — a sure cure for hunger or heartstabs, a prescription for joy, goodwill, and getting back your girl friend from any guy who buys her hamburgers down the street. In addition to the "burgers," you get a garnish tray. Please nod at the waiter.

1. **BURGER** 85
   With Lettuce, Tomato, Mayonnaise
2. **BURGER** 95
   Melted Cheese, Bacon, Lettuce, Tomato, Mayonnaise
3. **BURGER** 1.05
   Lettuce, Tomato, Mayonnaise, Fries
4. **BURGER** 1.15
   Melted Cheese, Bacon, Lettuce, Tomato, Mayonnaise, Fries
5. **BURGER** 1.25
   Melted Cheese, Bacon, Grilled Onion, Lettuce, Tomato, Mayonnaise, Fries

LUNCH AND DINNER

Includes a tossed green salad with your choice of dressing,
French fries, roll and beverage.

1. **HAMBURGER STEAK** 1.75
   A half pound of extra-lean beef, freshly ground and cooked to your order. Sliced tomato, pickle and carrot curl.
2. **FRIED BUTTERFLY SHRIMP** ...1.95
   Large, blue-water shrimp cooked to perfection — for you!
   Sliced tomato, pickle and carrot curl.

BEVERAGES

Coffee, Sanka, Tea (Hot) 20
Large Milk, Skimmed Milk, Chocolate Milk,
Buttermilk, Tea (Iced), Iced Coffee 20
Farrell's Special Hot Chocolate Covered with Whipped
Cream Served in a Turkish Cup 25

Farrell's Famous Ice Cream To Go 1.20 Qt.

Having a birthday — let Farrell's be your host
Ask About Our Birthday Package

**SEE OUR fountain menu above
for our ice cream extravaganzas**

DELICATESSEN SANDWICHES

All Farrell Sandwiches are prepared with the finest Grade A
Fancy Meats and Produce Available

1. **OLD TIME HOT CORNED BEEF** 1.35
   Served on Rye Bread with Dill Pickle, Carrot Curl, a Portion of Kraut to Add to Your Sandwich if Desired.
2. **NEW YORK HOT PASTRAMI** 1.25
   Served on Rye Bread with Dill Pickle, Carrot Curl, a Portion of Kraut to Add to Your Sandwich if Desired.
3. **DELICIOUS HOT BAKED HAM** 1.25
   Served on Rye Bread with Dill Pickle, Carrot Curl, a Portion of Kraut to Add to Your Sandwich if Desired.
4. **FRENCH DIP SANDWICH** 1.35
   Lean Beef Sliced Thin and Heaped High on Our French Roll.
   With Dill Pickle, Carrot Curl.

5. **REUBEN**

   Reuben once was in a fast game of Monopoly when someone complained about the food. Reuben, a dedicated cook (another word for bachelor), at that moment passed "Go," dashed to the kitchen, whomped up a sandwich which thrilled guests, who loaned Reuben $5,000 in a fit of generosity and Monopoly money*. (*Preceding info not documented) FARRELL'S subsequently improved the sandwich, to wit: We take two lavish slices of our own fresh rye bread, mound it high with a generous helping of tender corned beef, Swiss cheese, and a precise measurement of perfect sauerkraut, pop it onto our grill, and bear it proudly — hot, rich with flavor — to you.
   We call it "The Reuben." 1.70

6. **GRILLED CHEESE** 75
   Tasty American melted cheese served between bread grilled to a luscious golden brown.
   Served with Carrot Curl and Dill Pickle.
7. **BACON, LETTUCE & TOMATO** on Toast 85
   Served with Carrot Curl and Dill Pickle
8. **TASTY ROAST BEEF**   Served on White Bread, ..85
   Mayonnaise and Lettuce. Served with Carrot Curl and Dill Pickle.
9. **BAKED HAM & SWISS CHEESE** 1.35
   Served on Rye Bread with Dill Pickle and Side of Kraut. An Old Time Favorite Combination!
10. **GASTRONOMICAL DELICATESSEN-
    EPICUREAN'S DELIGHT** — WOW! 4.95
    This is a happening on an oven-fresh loaf of French Bread 14 inches long. What happens is a frenzied fantasy in which 10 wild little elves race up and down the sandwich board piling on corned beef; pastrami; ham; rich tasty roast beef; swiss cheese; crisp lettuce; red ripe tomatoes... An evening's eating for 1 to 4 people, depending on your appetite, and theirs!

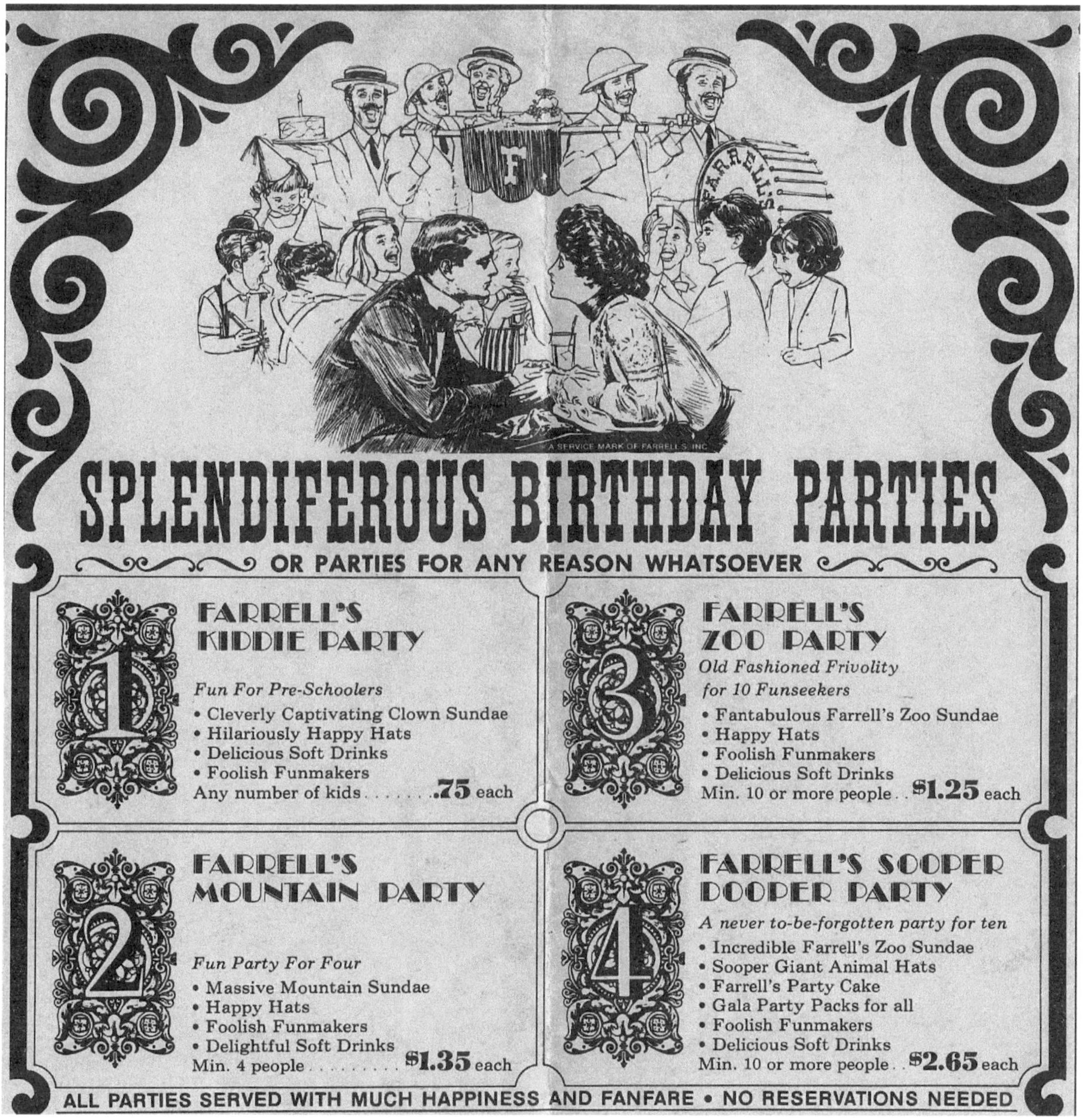

SPLENDIFEROUS BIRTHDAY PARTIES
OR PARTIES FOR ANY REASON WHATSOEVER

1. FARRELL'S KIDDIE PARTY
Fun For Pre-Schoolers
- Cleverly Captivating Clown Sundae
- Hilariously Happy Hats
- Delicious Soft Drinks
- Foolish Funmakers

Any number of kids......**.75** each

2. FARRELL'S MOUNTAIN PARTY
Fun Party For Four
- Massive Mountain Sundae
- Happy Hats
- Foolish Funmakers
- Delightful Soft Drinks

Min. 4 people........**$1.35** each

3. FARRELL'S ZOO PARTY
Old Fashioned Frivolity for 10 Funseekers
- Fantabulous Farrell's Zoo Sundae
- Happy Hats
- Foolish Funmakers
- Delicious Soft Drinks

Min. 10 or more people..**$1.25** each

4. FARRELL'S SOOPER DOOPER PARTY
A never to-be-forgotten party for ten
- Incredible Farrell's Zoo Sundae
- Sooper Giant Animal Hats
- Farrell's Party Cake
- Gala Party Packs for all
- Foolish Funmakers
- Delicious Soft Drinks

Min. 10 or more people..**$2.65** each

ALL PARTIES SERVED WITH MUCH HAPPINESS AND FANFARE • NO RESERVATIONS NEEDED

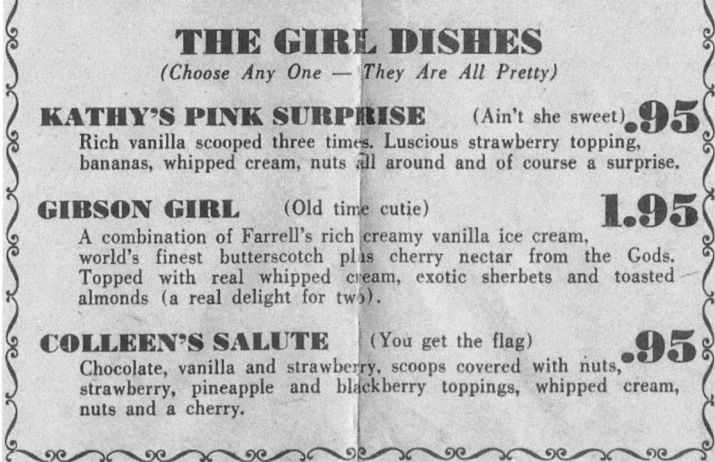

By 1974 and 1975 not much had changed in terms of menu design. The national menu did not use multi-color menus. Four party packages were offered for the kids, plus a special party package aimed at senior citizens. Spumoni ice cream was a thing of the past. A "Gay Nineties" sundae was added. The Hot Fudge Nutty-Nutty and Tin Roof were added to the menu. Price of a banana split - $1.25.

SUNDAES

FARRELL'S OLD FASHION SUNDAE .75
All sundaes include gobs of whipped cream, chocolate sprinkles, maraschino cherry and a wafer.
Chocolate   Strawberry   Butterscotch   Pineapple
Blackberry   Marshmallow
• Additional Syrup or Nuts on Sundaes 15c

HOT FUDGE SUNDAE .80
Two luscious scoops of our rich vanilla ice cream, pure whipped cream, toasted almonds, topped with a ruby red maraschino half and served with a steaming side of rich hot fudge for you to add as you go.

BLACK AND WHITE .85
Chocolate ice cream, marshmallow, vanilla ice cream, hot fudge, almonds, whipped cream and a cherry.

PARLOUR'S TIN ROOF .85
A foundation of thick hot fudge and salty spanish peanuts supports 2 scoops of Farrell's vanilla ice cream. Topped with more creamy hot fudge and a tin roof of more peanuts. A delicate cloud of whipped cream and a red cherry caresses this dish.

THE TROUGH Fit for a pig (You eat from the trough.) Special award if you eat this by yourself. Plenty for two — Just you and you. 2.15

PIKE'S PEAK (Climb this one.) Serves 1 - 4. 3.95
A mountain of rich vanilla, chocolate, strawberry, coffee and butter pecan ice cream with hot fudge slopes, topped with a marshmallow glacier, whipped cream, with a valley of bananas and strawberries below. (What a mess, but oh so good!) For groups over 4 we will make large mountains at 85c per head extra.

FARRELL'S ZOO (Divide it up, kids) 8.50
So huge it takes two strong men to deliver it to your table. Their knees sag under EIGHT flavors of our famous ice cream; THREE natural fruit flavor sherbets; FIVE different and delicious toppings; whipped cream; cherries; almonds and bananas. Additional servings 80c per person extra. Read about our Birthday package on the other side of this menu . . . it may be the most important reading you've ever done. (Serves one to ten.)

DELICATESSEN
SANDWICHES
(Served with Dill Pickle and Carrot Curl)

All Farrell's Sandwiches are prepared with the finest Grade A Fancy Meats and Produce Available

INSTANT (ALMOST) FEATURES
For Secretaries, Executives, Salesmen, Clerks, Doctors, and Indian Chiefs and Anyone else in a hurry.
Courageously Cool Cold Sandwiches

INCLUDES CHOICE OF SOUP OR SALAD AT **$1.25**
(Guaranteed to be served to you within 243½ seconds when ordered by your entire party.)

1. **OLD TIME CORNED BEEF**
FARRELL'S famous Iowa-Corn Fed Corned Beef piled high on Hearth-Baked Black Forest Rye Bread served with Lettuce and Tomato.

2. **COLD ROAST BEEF**
Roast Baron of Beef - medium - on our special white bread with Lettuce and Tomato.

3. **DELICIOUS BAKED HAM**
Sugar Cured Virginia Baked Ham served on Hearth-Baked Black Forest Rye Bread with Lettuce and Tomato.

ABOVE SANDWICHES ALA CARTE **$1.00**
(That's without soup or salad)

4. **REUBEN** We take two lavish slices of our own fresh rye bread, mound it high with a generous helping of tender corned beef, Swiss cheese, and a precise measurement of perfect sauerkraut, pop it into our grill, and bear it proudly — hot, rich with flavor — to you. We call it "The Reuben." **1.75**

5. **NEW YORK HOT PASTRAMI** 1.25
Served on Rye Bread with a Portion of Kraut to Add to Your Sandwich if Desired.

6. **TUNA SALAD** (We Use Only White Tuna) .... .85

7. **BACON, LETTUCE & TOMATO** on Toast .95

8. **COLD TURKEY, LETTUCE & TOMATO** .95

9. **EGG SALAD** —Piled High and Made to Order .... .85

10. **FRENCH DIP** 1.65
Thin Sliced Beef Piled High on Small French Loaf. Served with French Fries

LUNCH AND DINNER
Includes a tossed green salad with your choice of dressing, French fries, and a roll.

1. **HAMBURGER STEAK** 1.75
A half pound of extra-lean beef, freshly ground and cooked to your order. Sliced tomatoes, pickle and carrot curl.

2. **FRIED BUTTERFLY SHRIMP** 2.25
Large, blue-water shrimp cooked to perfection—for you! Sliced tomatoes, pickle and carrot curl. (5 Shrimp)

3. **FISH AND CHIPS** 1.75
An old time favorite — batter dipped Icelandic Cod. Sliced tomatoes, pickle and carrot curl.

4. **LOW CALORIE - DIET PLATE** 1.25
¼ lb. pure ground beef pattie, farm fresh cottage cheese, sliced garden tomato, thinly sliced carrot curl, Ry-Krisp crackers, garnished with a sprig of no-cal parsley.

Gay Ninety Sundae
For our lunch and dinner customers we offer our ever-popular single scoop "Gay Ninety" sundae. Strawberry, Chocolate, Blackberry and Butterscotch. .45

KIDDIES MENU
10 AND UNDER
(Also 65 and over)

KIDDIE HANGERBER	.65
EGG SALAD SAMICH	.50
CHEESE SAMICH	.50
PEANUT BUTTER & JELLY SAMICH	.50
CLOWN SUNDAE - Chocolate or Strawberry	.35
LITTLE SHAKES - Chocolate or Strawberry	.35
LITTLE SODAS - Chocolate or Strawberry	.35

BABY BOTTLES WARMED
And Any Special Food We Can Prepare for Your Youngster Please Ask
15c Extra for Grilled Sandwiches

BEVERAGES and SIDE ORDERS

Tossed Green Salad (Your Favorite Dressing)	.45
Side of French Fries (Shoestring Style)	.35
Soup of the Day Cup .35 Lg. Bowl	.65
Our Famous Chili (Cooked Slowly with Lean Meat and Plump Red Beans) Cup .40 Lg. Bowl	.75
Coffee, Sanka, Iced Coffee, Tea (Hot), Tea (Iced)	.20
Extra Large Milk, Skimmed Milk, Chocolate Milk and Buttermilk	.25
Farrell's Special Hot Chocolate covered with Whipped Cream served in a Turkish Cup	.25

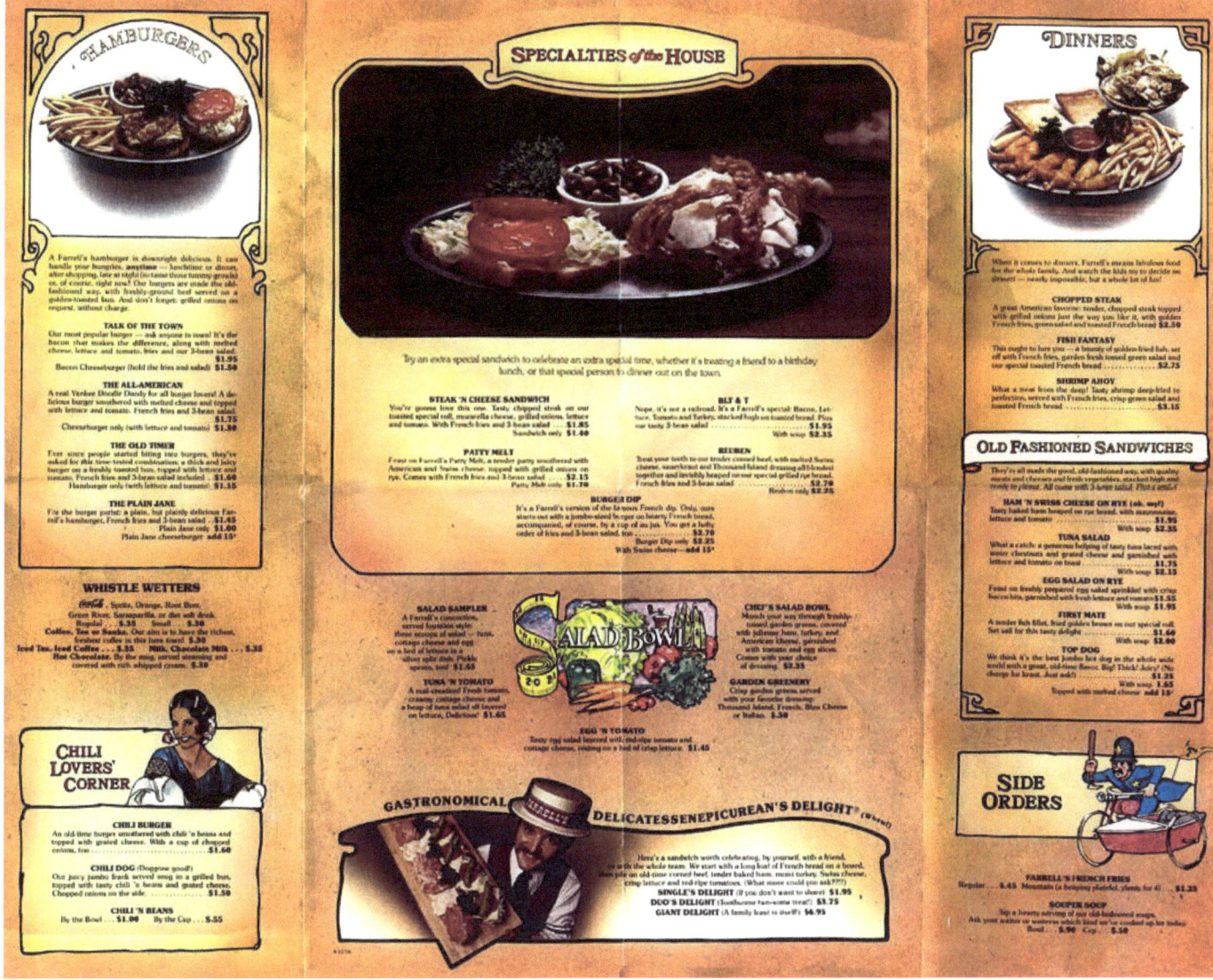

1976

Burgers got fancy names - the Bacon Cheeseburger became the "Talk of the Town", the Hamburger became the "Old Timer," etc.

More salads were offered on this menu including Tuna 'n Tomato, and Egg 'n Tomato.

The Hot Fudge Cake, Gold Mine and Strawberry Surprise were born on this menu.

The 1976 Farrell's menu would be upscaled to a glossy, full-color, tri-fold menu with new and higher-quality food items, replacing the traditional newsprint style.

TALK OF THE TOWN
Our most popular burger — ask anyone in town! It's the *bacon* that makes the difference, along with melted cheese, lettuce and tomato, fries and our 3-bean salad.
$1.95
Bacon Cheeseburger (hold the fries and salad) $1.50

THE ALL-AMERICAN
A real Yankee Doodle Dandy for all burger lovers! A delicious burger smothered with melted cheese and topped with lettuce and tomato. French fries and 3-bean salad.
$1.75
Cheeseburger only (with lettuce and tomato) $1.30

THE OLD TIMER
Ever since people started biting into burgers, they've asked for *this* time-tested combination: a thick and juicy burger on a freshly toasted bun, topped with lettuce and tomato. French fries and 3-bean salad included ..$1.60
Hamburger only (with lettuce and tomato) $1.15

THE PLAIN JANE
For the burger purist: a plain, but plainly delicious Farrell's hamburger, French fries and 3-bean salad ..$1.45
Plain Jane only $1.00
Plain Jane cheeseburger **add 15¢**

FARRELL'S
DINING & ICE CREAM PARLOUR

What makes Farrell's unique? What brings folks back time and again? One big reason is the old-fashioned value you find in everything we serve, from our ice cream creations to our fabulous food. But mostly it's our people that sets us apart. Bright, friendly gals and guys who really (truly!) enjoy helping you have a great time. No wonder Farrell's is fun for everyone. For lovers mooning over a treat for two in their own special corner. For weary shoppers looking for a little relief (Farrell's is one place they'll always find a welcome smile). For all kinds of people celebrating all kinds of things: team victories, anniversaries, you name it! For families—because Farrell's is like a home away from home. No fancy duds required. No being extra quiet. Just fun, friendship, and the best food in town next to Mom's.

And not a day goes by without a Farrell's birthday party, complete with cakes and mob-sized sundaes all wrapped up with grins and a roomful of song. (We've even got special birthday packages. Just ask our cashier.)

Yep. To just about everyone who's ever visited us, Farrell's is an extra special sort of place. And we do our best to keep it that way. All of us feel that, just by being in business, we've made a promise to each and every customer: you must be satisfied. So, if we ever let you down, please let us know. Because without you, we are nothing.

ON YOUR BIRTHDAY, THE SUNDAE IS ON US (FREE!)

Just tell the waiter it's your day, and make a wish. And don't forget to ask the cashier about our special birthday parties. After all. Nobody knows as much about fabulous fun as Farrell's.

HOT FUDGE SUNDAES

THE SUPER PURIST
Just the ticket for the true Hot Fudge Fanatic—no whipped cream, no nuts, just lots and lots of rich vanilla ice cream and a large pitcher of gooey hot fudge. Pure goodness . . . $2.75

TRIPLE TREAT (Just right)
Three scoops of vanilla ice cream, topped with 2 cups of our rich hot fudge, whipped cream, toasted almonds and a cherry. You'll love it! . . . $1.50

ORIGINAL HOT FUDGE
Two scoops of rich vanilla ice cream, plus a steaming side of our famous hot fudge, whipped cream, toasted almonds and a cherry . . . $1.10

BLACK AND WHITE
What a combination! Rich chocolate ice cream topped with creamy marshmallow and vanilla ice cream smothered with hot fudge. Plus whipped cream, toasted almonds and a cherry . . . $1.00

NUTS 'N' NUTS

HOT FUDGE NUTTY NUTTY
Three scoops of magnificent vanilla ice cream covered with nuts galore—toasted almonds and crunchy, old-time Spanish peanuts topped with whipped cream and a cherry. Accompanied by not just one, but two cups of thick hot fudge to give you the fudgiest, nuttiest sundae ever scooped! . . . $1.75

PARLOUR'S TIN ROOF
A foundation of thick hot fudge and salty Spanish peanuts support two scoops of Farrell's vanilla ice cream. Topped with more creamy fudge, a tin roof of peanuts, a creamy cloud of whipped cream, and a cherry . . . $1.10

OLD FASHIONED SUNDAES

Luscious Farrell's vanilla ice cream topped with real whipped cream, chocolate sprinkles and a cherry (plus a wafer, too, just for you!) Choice of the following toppings:

Chocolate	Blackberry	Butterscotch
Pineapple	Strawberry	Marshmallow

Banana Slices . . . 10¢ extra

SUPER SCOOP SUNDAE
It's super-sized. Super good! Three scoops of ice cream, with your choice of topping, whipped cream, chocolate sprinkles and a cherry . . . $1.35

ANY DAY SUNDAE
Our two scoop sundae made with rich ice cream and all the trimmings. Good today or any day . . . $.95

CAKE A LA MODE

GOLD MINE
Talk about striking it rich! Two slices of big, moist white cake with butter pecan ice cream sandwiched in between. Topped with hot butterscotch, whipped cream and a cherry . . . $1.25

HOT FUDGE CAKE
Two slices of delicious devil's food cake with vanilla ice cream sandwiched in between, plus hot fudge topping, whipped cream and a cherry. Heavenly! . . . $1.25

STRAWBERRY SURPRISE
We start with 2 slices of our white cake, then add vanilla ice cream, strawberry topping and whipped cream. Plus a cherry! . . . $1.25

LUNCHEON SUNDAES

LUNCHEON HOT FUDGE
Farrell's ice cream topped with rich hot fudge. Just the right size for less-than-famished Hot Fudge feasters! . . . $.70

LUNCHEON OLD FASHIONED
Rich ice cream with your choice of toppings, plus all the old-fashioned trimmings . . . $.60

BANANA SPLITS

TWO FOR THE ROAD
Our super-sized banana split served in a special trough. Plenty for two. Or, if it's just you and you, eat it by yourself, and we'll throw in a special award! . . . $2.50

ALL-AMERICAN BANANA SPLIT
The Flagship of Farrell's Fleet. Chocolate, vanilla and strawberry ice cream, smothered in splendiferous toppings, crowned with whipped cream and toasted almonds. And of course, a banana . . . $1.45

ROYALE SUNDAES

BANANA FUDGE ROYALE
Fit for a king or queen! Two scoops of vanilla ice cream, split banana, topped with whipped cream, toasted almonds, a cherry, plus a gleaming cup of our thick, hot fudge. You'll go bananas! . . . $1.25

STRAWBERRY ROYALE
A sweet treat! Two scoops of vanilla ice cream, strawberry topping, split banana, whipped cream, toasted almonds and a cherry . . . $1.25

GOLDDIGGER ROYALE
You'll be in a happy vein with two scoops of scrumptious butter pecan ice cream beneath a luscious lode of hot butterscotch topping, with a tasty split banana, whipped cream, toasted almonds and a cherry. Strike it rich! . . . $1.25

APPLE PANDOWDY ROYALE
It's a goody! Two scoops of Farrell's vanilla ice cream covered with spicy sliced apples, golden crunch surrounded by a split banana and topped with rich whipped cream and a cherry . . . $1.25

SHAKES & SODAS
FREEZES 'N FLOATS, TOO

SHAKES AND SODAS

SHAKES
An all-time favorite. Thick! Rich! Creamy!

Vanilla	Chocolate Mint	Root Beer
Chocolate	Coffee Mocha	Butterscotch
Strawberry	Cherry	Pineapple

Small Shake . . . $.75
Super Shake (A fountain favorite) . . . $.90
Super Duper Shake
(Extra large, served in our Super Duper glass!) $1.25
With old-fashioned malt 5¢ extra With banana 20¢ extra

SODAS
So good, they're guaranteed — the sodas with zip or we make 'em over.

Vanilla	Coffee	Choffee
Chocolate	Cherry	(Chocolate soda
Strawberry	Root Beer	with Coffee ice cream)
Chocolate Mint	Pineapple	Bob Farrell's favorite

Small Soda $.75 Super Soda $.90
Super Duper Soda. Three scoops of m-m-magnificent ice cream, plus a glass of soda water. And wait 'til you see the glass! . . . $1.25

FREEZES (To cool you) Our Super Freezes come in three frosty-fresh flavors: raspberry, orange or lime . . . $.80

ICE CREAM FLOATS A real old-time treat — your favorite flavor of ice cream and soda. Coca-Cola, Root Beer or Sprite . . . $.60
Super Duper 3-scoop floats . . . $1.10 Sodawater (plain) . . . 2¢

ICE CREAM & SHERBET

We serve up rich, old-time barrel-scrapin' ice cream made from our own special recipes. We pride ourselves on our quality —it's outstanding!

Vanilla	Peppermint	Lime Sherbet	OLD-TIME
Strawberry	Butter Pecan	Raspberry Sherbet	SLAB
Chocolate	Coffee	Orange Sherbet	$.60
Chocolate Chip Mint			

COLOSSAL CREATIONS

GIBSON GIRL
A beautiful combination of Farrell's creamy vanilla ice cream, rich butterscotch, and cherry nectar from the gods. It's topped with whipped cream, exotic sherbets and toasted almonds. A real delight for two! . . . $1.95

PIKE'S PEAK
A mountain of rich vanilla, chocolate, strawberry, coffee and butter pecan ice cream with hot fudge slopes, topped with a marshmallow glacier, whipped cream, with a valley of bananas and strawberry topping below. (A mighty big mess, but oh, so good!) Serves 1 to 4 . . . $4.40
For groups over 4, we'll make larger mountains at $1.10 per person extra

THE ZOO
So huge, it takes two strong men to deliver it to your table. Their knees sag under SEVEN flavors of our famous ice cream, THREE fruit flavor sherbets, FIVE different and delicious toppings, plus whipped cream, cherries, toasted almonds and bananas. Serves 1 to 10 . . . $9.95
Additional servings per person $1.00 extra.

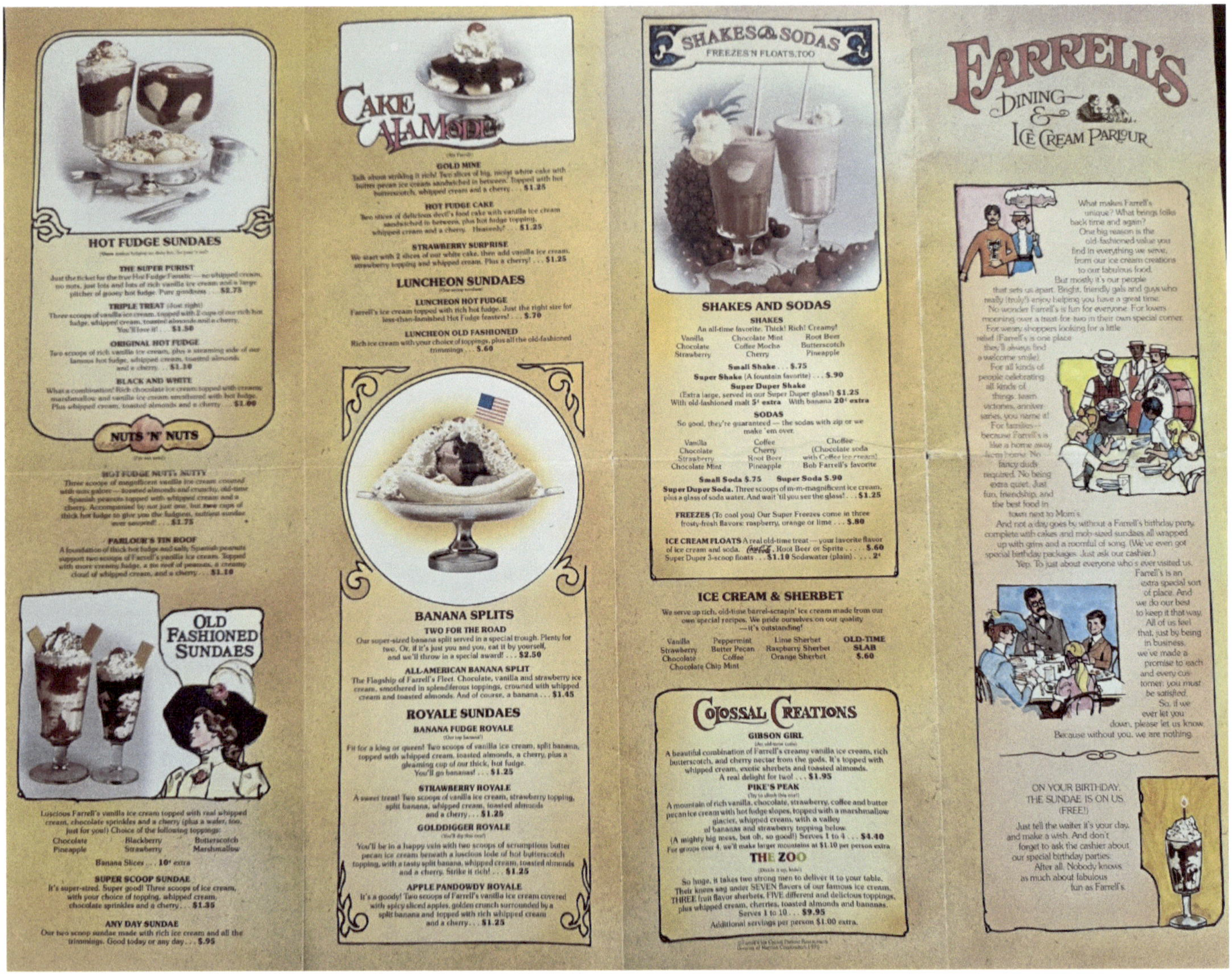

1976

The Trough sundae was renamed "Two for the Road." The Hot Fudge Cake, Gold Mine and Strawberry Surprise were born on this menu. The price of a banana split was $1.45.

OLD FASHIONED SUNDAES

Luscious Farrell's vanilla ice cream topped with real whipped cream, chocolate sprinkles and a cherry (plus a wafer, too, just for you!) Choice of the following toppings:

Chocolate	Blackberry	Butterscotch
Pineapple	Strawberry	Marshmallow

COLOSSAL CREATIONS

GIBSON GIRL
(An old-time cutie)
A beautiful combination of Farrell's creamy vanilla ice cream, rich butterscotch, and cherry nectar from the gods. It's topped with whipped cream, exotic sherbets and toasted almonds. A real delight for two! . . . $1.95

PIKE'S PEAK
(Try to climb this one!)
A mountain of rich vanilla, chocolate, strawberry, coffee and butter pecan ice cream with hot fudge slopes, topped with a marshmallow glacier, whipped cream, with a valley of bananas and strawberry topping below. (A mighty big mess, but oh, so good!) Serves 1 to 4 . . . $4.40
For groups over 4, we'll make larger mountains at $1.10 per person extra

THE ZOO
(Divide it up, kids!)
So huge, it takes two strong men to deliver it to your table. Their knees sag under SEVEN flavors of our famous ice cream, THREE fruit flavor sherbets, FIVE different and delicious toppings, plus whipped cream, cherries, toasted almonds and bananas. Serves 1 to 10 . . . $9.95
Additional servings per person $1.00 extra.

©Farrell's Ice Cream Parlour Restaurants
Division of Marriott Corporation 1976

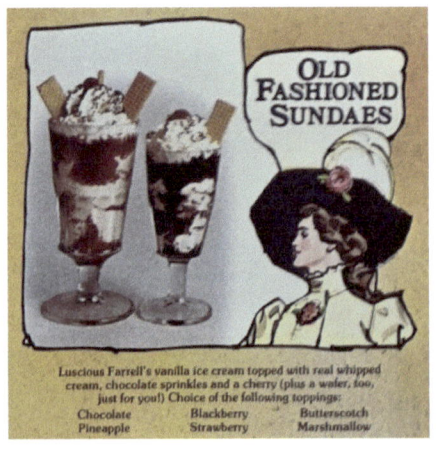

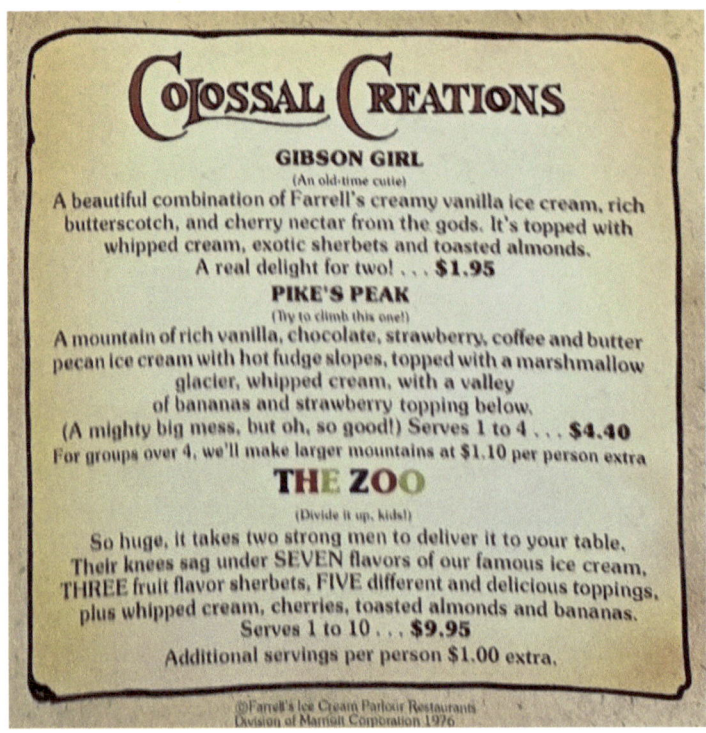

Farrell's is an extra special sort of place. And we do our best to keep it that way. All of us feel that, just by being in business, we've made a promise to each and every customer: you must be satisfied. So, if we ever let you down, please let us know. Because without you, we are nothing.

BANANA SPLITS

TWO FOR THE ROAD
Our super-sized banana split served in a special trough. Plenty for two. Or, if it's just you and you, eat it by yourself, and we'll throw in a special award! . . . $2.50

ALL-AMERICAN BANANA SPLIT
The Flagship of Farrell's Fleet. Chocolate, vanilla and strawberry ice cream, smothered in splendiferous toppings, crowned with whipped cream and toasted almonds. And of course, a banana . . . $1.45

The **1979** menu, at left, was introduced as a two-color menu that reduced the six columns of food and fountain offerings into three columns. The "Keystone Cop" graphics were replaced. The menu had only several changes, including the first time offering of ice cream puffs. A "Rocky Road" was added. The Hot Fudge Volcano made its debut with thirty scoops of vanilla ice cream and a 20-ounce goblet of hot fudge. A sundae called "Our Accountant's Favorite" was put on the menu. Banana split - $2.

SUNDAE SAMPLERS

Our Accountant's Favorite $99.00
A perfectly round scoop of vanilla ice cream on a perfectly smooth white plate. A dab of marshmallow topping. (Our accountant's kind of wild.) $99.00 plus tax. No small bills please.

This 1982 menu, at left and below, is courtesy of John Guest, Christopher's, Inc. It is similar in many ways to the 1982 menu on the next page from the Hawaiian franchise on Kauai. Prices ran about 35 to 45 percent more on the menu in Hawaii due to shipping costs. Plain soda water was still two cents. The menu noted - "No substitutions. Survivors will be prosecuted." Sides of hot fudge was 50 cents in the mainland and 95 cents in Hawaii. Banana Split - $2.60.

1982 According to Roger Baker, "This menu is from the Hawaiian franchise on Kauai. The Hawaiian parlours reflected the character of the islands, and the menus provided some of the unique items. Since nearly everything had to be shipped from the mainland, prices were usually at least 35% higher than the continental menus." Some of the features of this menu include burgers and sandwiches that were offered with a choice of french fries or white rice.

A special food section called "Island Favorites" featured such items as Teriyaki Beef, Hawaiian Fruit Salad, and Saimin, a "traditional hot Island soup with noodles, bits of ham, parsley, and broth." Also, Madam Pele's Volcano was the Kauai version of the Hot Fudge Volcano.

1982 Kauai Menu continued:

"A franchise special, Luna's Favorite, was offered with choice of carrot cake or hot fudge brownie, topped with vanilla ice cream.

The Top Banana sundae was offered. This sundae was on menus nationally for a year or so. There were 30 scoops of vanilla, chocolate and strawberry ice cream, five bananas, lots of strawberry, chocolate and pineapple topping plus the usual whipped cream, almonds and cherries in a big bowl. The public greeted this monstrosity with wild indifference.

Price of a banana split in Hawaii - $3.95.

1983 The "Impact 83" menu.

Roger Baker notes on his web site "that this menu was rolled out in November 1983 to all company parlours. This menu had four pages of food items, with ice cream relegated to the back two pages (plus a fold-out tab). Notable items included:

A New York strip steak dinner was offered. Basket Meals were offered, including the Vegetable Combo, Chicken Strips, Fried Shrimp, and a Deli Sampler."

"The Gastronomicaldelicatessenepicurean's Delight was renamed the Deli Special.

Nothing notable happened on the sundae menu. In May 1984, the salad bars in company parlours were eliminated. New salads were added to the menu including a Taco Salad, Tuna Salad, Chef's Salad, and Cobb Salad. The price of a banana split was $2.95. In December 1984, a smaller but similar appearing menu was rolled out, which eliminated 80% of all food items (leaving only five hamburgers, a club sandwich, grilled chicken sandwich and a salad offering). Ice cream offerings were increased, adding a number of six scoop sundaes such as the Black & Tan, Hot Butterscotch Delight, Marshmallow Fudge, and Super Fudge Sundaes. The Pig's Trough was doubled in size from six scoops to twelve scoops."

1985 *(part 1)*

"While company-owned parlours went through menu gyrations, most franchisees stayed the course with the paper menu and associated offerings." This menu is from the San Diego franchisee, which was still operating four parlours at the time. The following are offerings that were unique to this franchise -

Polish Dog Sandwich, Bar BQ Beef Sandwich, and America's Finest City Sundae (Created by Becky Waer.) It consisted of strawberry ice cream, blackberry topping, whipped cream, chocolate sprinkles and a cherry." (As described by Roger Baker.)

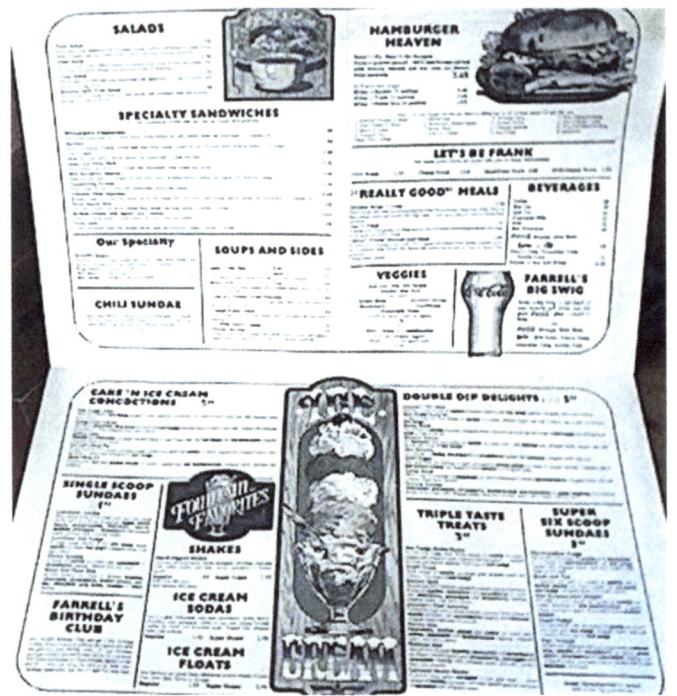

1985 *(part 2)*

The paper menu returned to company-owned parlours after a two-year absence. Food items were returned to the menu after a short absence as well. The Pig's Trough came back to its classic six-scoop architecture. Prices were also adjusted on items to provide more value to the customer. The Banana Split Fruit Salad debuted in this menu, as did the Chili Sundae.

> Farrell's version of Build-Your-Own-Burger was unveiled, where the customer could pick their choice of 16 toppings to add to the burger (at $.30 each). Some of the stranger toppings included chopped almonds, peanut butter & jelly, and banana slices. Fresh hamburgers went away, replaced with frozen patties (although this time the patties were a special product produced for one of Marriott's other restaurant divisions, and it actually tasted good).
>
> Ana Banana replaced the Fudge-Ana and Straw-Ana. The Ana Banana offered a choice of toppings, including Blackberrry.
>
> Price of a banana split - $2.85. This menu style was the last company issued menu. (Roger Baker.)

2001

The Farrell's franchisee in San Diego had been operating parlours continually since 1968. This menu is from late 2001. The quarter fold style opens to an inside which takes the best of the early menus.

Food offerings were numerous and over-the-top with "Krabby Cake" burgers, Bacon Cheeseburger with Avocado, and Chinese Chicken Salad.

Unique sundae offerings on this menu included Mudslides, S'More, Monkeyshines, and Black Forest.

Rocky Road and Chocolate Chip were available as ice cream flavors.

Price of a Banana Split - $5.65.

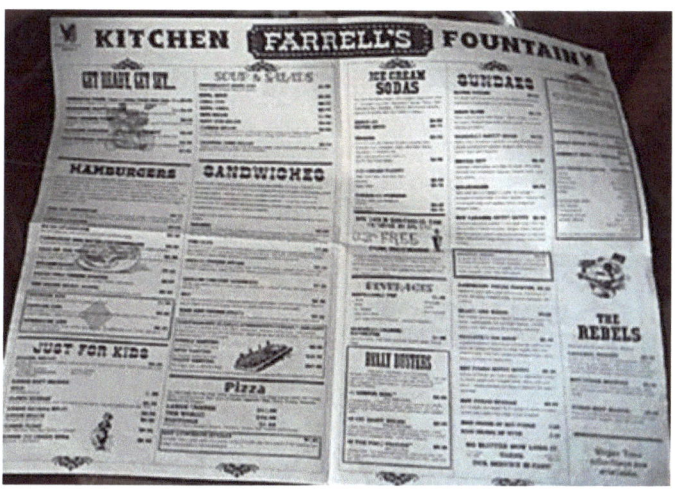

2002

The first parlour opened by Parlour Enterprises used this menu. Fairly balanced between food and fountain items, the following items were well known.

Pizza was originally offered by company-owned free-standing parlours from 1979 through 1982. Pizza was popular with kids, so it was widely sold with the party packages.

The Gastronomicaldelicatessenepicurean's Delight gets it full name back after nearly two decades.

Slugger burgers - the west coast did not have the "White Castle" chain, so this was the closest to a 'slider' that one had in California.

A "Build-your-own" sundae section was offered.

The Zoo sundae was notably absent from the ala-carte menu (although it is referenced in the party section on the back page).

Price of a Banana Split - $6.25

(As provided by Roger Baker.)

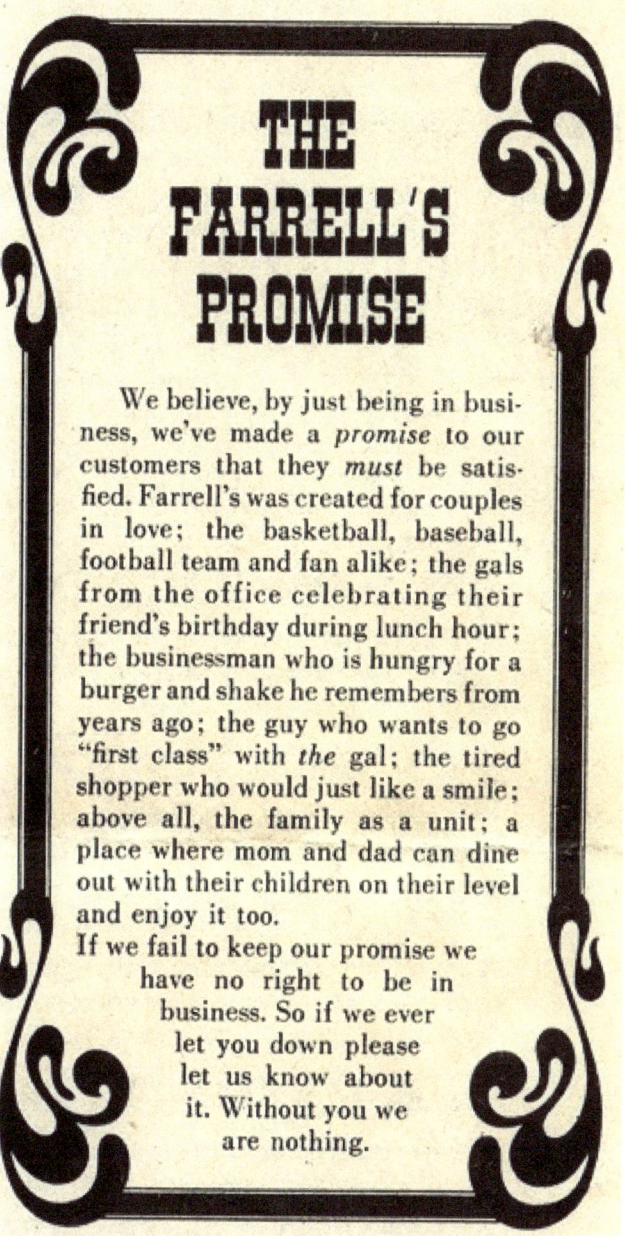

Special thanks to Roger Baker for maintaining a historic, written record of Farrell's menus and changes through the years. Thank you for sharing this valuable history with all of us.

FARRELL'S BRINGS ICE CREAM PARLOUR RESTAURANTS BACK TO ALL AMERICA

Things used to be different. Families used to enjoy good clean fun together. Boys and girls used to make eyes at each other over their favorite treat at the drugstore. And dates didn't cost a mint of money. Everyone thought life was just grand. Of course, that was a long time ago—way back in the days when soda fountains outnumbered bars in just about every town in the U.S.

When prohibition came, Ice Cream Parlours went into the food business and became even funner as Parlour Restaurants.

Suddenly, prohibition was at an end and food returned to the cocktail restaurant, ice cream went to drugstores and later to supermarkets. Mark the temporary demise of the good old-fashioned Family Parlour Restaurant. Good, clean fun (sob, sob) had no place to go.

Until a man named Bob Farrell came along.

FABULOUS FARRELL'S
GOOD ICE CREAM
GOOD FOOD
GOOD TIMES

You ought to meet Bob Farrell. He looks like a man out of another generation—the happy days of yore when complexions were ruddy, moustaches groomed and smiles were toothy. Bob's the man who brought back the good old Ice Cream Parlour Restaurants. He did it with an unbeatable formula of fantastic fountain fantasies, fabulous food, frolicking fun-filled surroundings and atmosphere and family type wholesomeness.

Everything about Farrell's is authentic. Bob Farrell wouldn't have it any other way. From the black and white checkerboard floor, to the bright red flocked wallpaper, to the Tiffany lamps and the bentwood chairs, Farrell's takes you back into a past generation that was leisurely and full of fabulous frolicsome fun. Even the people at Farrell's are genuine—the kind of people you'd like living next door to you.

The Farrell's Promise, written by Bob Farrell himself, sums up what you can look forward to every time you visit America's #1 Ice Cream Parlour.

FARRELL'S ICE CREAM PARLOUR RESTAURANTS

FOLLOW THIS LOW CALORIE DIET MENU AND EAT ALL THE ICE CREAM YOU WANT!

MONDAY
Breakfast: Weak Tea
Lunch: (1) Bouillon Cube in Half Cup Diluted Water
Dinner: One Pigeon Thigh; Three Ounces Prune Juice (gargle only)

TUESDAY
Breakfast: Scraped Crumbs From Burnt Toast
Lunch: One Doughnut Hole (without sugar) One Glass of Dehydrated Water
Dinner: Three Grains Cornmeal Broiled

WEDNESDAY
Breakfast: Shredded Egg Shell Skin
Lunch: One-Half Dozen Poppy Seeds
Dinner: Bee's Knees and Mosquito Knuckles Sauteed in Vinegar

THURSDAY
Breakfast: Boiled Out Stains of Old Table Cloth
Lunch: Belly Button of a Navel Orange
Dinner: Three Eyes From Irish Potato (Diced)

FRIDAY
Breakfast: Two Lobster Antennas
Lunch: One Tail Joint of Sea Horse
Dinner: Rotisserie Broiled Guppy Filet

SATURDAY
Breakfast: Four Chopped Banana Seeds
Lunch: Broiled Butterfly Liver
Dinner: Jelly Vertebrae a la Centipede

SUNDAY
Breakfast: Pickled Humming Bird Tongue
Lunch: Prime Rib of Tadpole; Aroma of Empty Custard Pie Plate
Dinner: Tossed Paprika and Clover Leaf Salad

NOTE: A 7-ounce glass of steam may be consumed alternate days to help in having something to blow off.

Anything Worth Eating Has Calories!

VISIT ALL OF FARRELL'S RESTAURANTS, LOCATED THROUGHOUT AMERICA
See other side for listing

Copyright © Farrell's, Inc. 1966-1971

When Jeff and Jan Zorn brought Jen and Ren to visit the Brea, California Farrell's in late 2018, little did they know that Jeff would capture photographs of one of the last menus in the history of Farrell's Ice Cream Parlours. Peaking over the kitchen side of the menu, above, is a fascinated Jen. At left, she is reviewing the other side of the menu with the fountain treats.

History of the ICE CREAM PARLOUR RESTAURANT

NOTORIOUS NERO FATHERS FOUNTAIN FANTASIES

Believe it or not, the idea that eventually led to the fabulous Ice Cream Parlour Restaurant as we know it today actually started way back in the first century with that famous fiddling fellow, Emperor Nero...who used to send fleets of slaves to the mountains for ice and snow to freeze the fruit drinks he favored.

Marco Polo got into the act when he brought back from the Orient a recipe for making water ices, which the Asians had enjoyed for thousands of years.

Some 300 years ago, along came Charles the First of England, who was so delighted with his cook's cool concoction featuring a frozen cream ice desert that he pensioned him with 500 pounds a year to restrict the recipe to the royal table. (See...our fountain fizzicians have *great* futures!)

Today, of course, that delicious delicacy known as "ice cream" has spread to the four corners of the world. Leave it to Nero to come up with a hot item from a cool confection!

ICE CREAM CONE BECOMES FAIR FAVORITE

A surprise hit of the St. Louis World's Fair in 1904 was an interesting and edible container of ice cream. Strangely enough, this incredible idea was called the "ice cream cone."

This tasty treat has proved popular with youngsters and oldsters alike to this very day...as many as 2,500,000,000 are sold every year!

BUSINESS BOOM SEES SODA SUCCESS

A man by the name of John Matthews introduced carbonated water to the citizenry in 1833. Syrups were added a few years later by a Frenchman and, in 1874, a concessionaire who ran out of flavoring for his soda water during the noon rush served it with a scoop of ice cream and the ice cream soda was born.

Some years later, prohibitionists in Evanston, Illinois declared soda water intoxicating and decided sodas could not be served on Sunday. An ingenious drug store operator located a legal loophole allowing perpetuation of his profits...he simply served ice cream and syrup, leaving out the soda water, and the "Sunday" was invented! The spelling was later changed when town fathers objected...and that's how a soda became a Sundae.

(If *your* Sundae hasn't arrived yet, keep reading.)

A SAD STORY WITH A HAPPY ENDING

Once upon a time there was good, clean fun. Families enjoyed it together. Boys and girls shared it on dates. People thought life was grand. Of course, that was a long time ago...back in the days when there were more soda fountains than bars in New York City!

When prohibition came in, saloons went out and so did their tasty food combinations. Ice cream parlors soon started serving food and became even more popular as Parlour Restaurants. Good clean fun was even funner!

But alas, with the end of prohibition food went back to the cocktail restaurants and ice cream went to the drug stores and later, supermarkets. Sad to say, the good old Family Parlour Restaurant faded away. Good clean fun (sob) had no place to go.

Now for the happy ending. One year not so long ago a happy fellow named Bob Farrell, who even looked like he belonged in those happy days of yore, brought the good old Ice Cream Parlour Restaurant back! He really did, with an unbeatable formula of fabulous food 'n fantastic fountain fantasies for frolicking fun-filled festive families!

Now families are together again! Boys are dating girls again! People think life is grand again...and it is!

Hurrah for good clean fun...and no better way to enjoy it than a party at FARRELL'S!

Thank you to everyone who submitted photographs and information for this chapter on Farrell's menus. Without their help, there may not have been a written record of the Farrell's menus for over 50 years to preserve and share. Thanks to Roger Baker, Mike Fleming, Paul Kramer, Marcus Lemonis, Mark Murphy, Tom Ortman, Howard A. Sutherland, and Jeff Zorn.

Also, for several high-resolution, full menus covering multiple years, thank you to John Guest, Christopher's Inc., Santa Ana, California. Thanks to the Wikipedia website.

Birthday Parties and Family Fun

Hot Fudge Volcano

Birthday party package ad from Southfield, Michigan (Courtesy of Dan Barth.)

At Farrell's, through the years, it was all about the smiles and fun for kids of all ages. (Courtesy of John Ortman, Mike Fleming, Paul Kramer, Farrell's USA, and others.)

One year old Aaron Schwartz celebrates his birthday in the Southfield, Michigan Farrell's, 1976. Below, with Grandpa Max Lebow. At right with dad, Jack. (Courtesy of Aaron Schwartz.)

Above, the birthday party for 6-year-old Jon Nachman at the Southfield, Michigan Farrell's in 1972. Mom Marilyn, at left helping to serve Jon's friends. (Courtesy of Jonathan Nachman.)

Whether you were with a group (right) or by yourself (left), Farrell's brought out the smiles and helped make you feel special. (1973)

Below, Farrell's participated in a Kid's birthday party competition and was one of three finalists, per readers. Server Daniel Chavez holds a tray full of ice cream creations. (Best of OC, Orange County Register.)

Above, celebrating Jennifer Cutler's 10th birthday at Farrell's in Southfield, Michigan. From left are Estelle Herman Wendzinski, Aida Cutler (Jennifer and Wendy's mom), Jennifer (in the red), and Wendy Cutler Luczak.

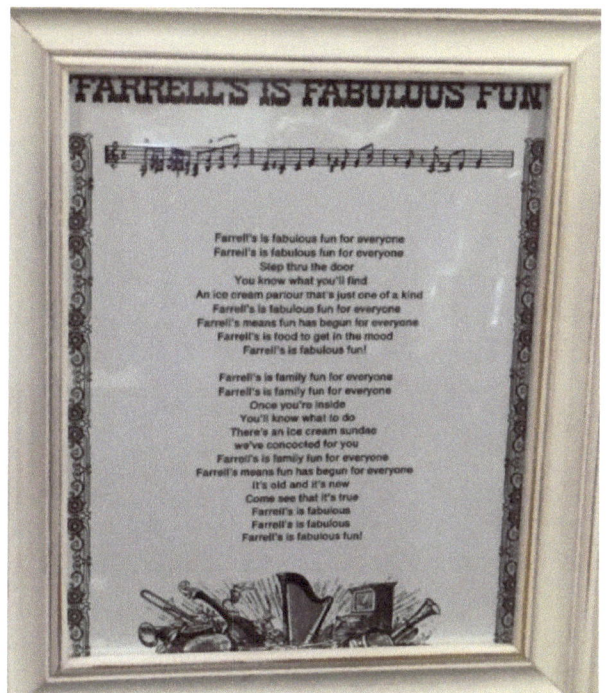

"FARRELL'S IS FABULOUS FUN"

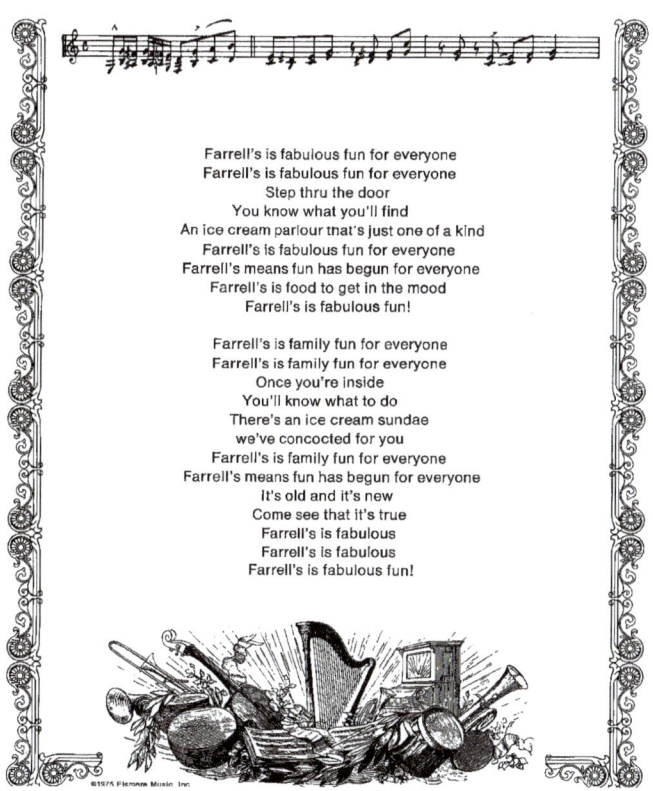

In addition to the "Happy Birthday Song," Farrell's also had a theme song called "Farrell's Is Fabulous Fun." The music sheets appear on the next two pages. Words and music are by Steve Karmen.

The 'Happy Birthday to You' song was the reason parents brought their children to Farrell's, in addition to the draw of the free sundae. This song is known the world over and may be sung thousands of times every day. It was composed by Mildred J Hill, a schoolteacher born in Louisville KY on June 27, 1859, along with her younger sister, Patty Smith Hill, who wrote the lyrics for the later version.

Mildred J. Hill (Wikipedia.)

Farrell's Is Fabulous Fun

FARRELL'S ICE CREAM PARLOURS

Words and Music by
STEVE KARMEN

(If *your* Sundae hasn't arrived yet, keep reading.)

Below, Celina Solomon, while attending Chapman University in California, was treated to dinner and a sundae for her birthday at the Farrell's in Brea by her parents, Robert (shown at the door on the way in) and Susan Solomon. Everyone enjoyed the service, the attention, and being treated to the Happy Birthday song by the waitstaff, at right. (Photos by Robert Solomon.)

Marcus Lemonis, then owner of Farrell's, received a happy birthday greeting on the Farrell's Facebook page, November 16, 2016. Shauna Parisi, center, looking on. They also posted the caption, "A special Birthday shout out to Marcus Lemonis! Happy Birthday, Mr. Lemonis!"

POLICE FORCE PARTY

($3.85 each)

It's what most kids dream of. A police force just for them! Only at Farrell's.
* Party hot dog or grilled cheese sandwich.
* French fries
* Clown sundae delivered to your table by Captain Birthday and the fun enforcement officers.
* Coke
* Stick-on moustache.
* Farrell's Police Force I.D. wallet & coupon
* Free Police hat for birthday boy or girl with a party of 10 or more. (Additional hats $2.25 each.)
* Colorful helium balloons
* Souvenir certificate dedicated to the guest of honor and suitable for framing.
* No mess to clean up for Mom or Dad.

(Without hot dog, sandwich or fries: $2.85 each.)
Tip not included

ZOO PARTY

Minimum of 10 Fun Seekers ($4.00 each)
* Party hot dog or grilled cheese sandwich
* French fries
* The one and only Farrell's Fantastic Zoo perched on a stretcher and run through the jungle to your table by a pair of brave Farrell's zookeepers. (You know it's a zoo by the roar of bells, sirens, drums...). You'll need a ferocious appetite for this wild mix of 5 ice creams, 3 sherbets, 5 toppings, whipped cream, nuts, cherries, and bananas.
* Coke
* Birthday Hat
* Party Favor
* Colorful helium balloons
* Souvenir certificate dedicated to the guest of honor, and suitable for framing
* No mess to clean up.

(Without hot dog, sandwich or fries: $3.00 each.)
Tip not included

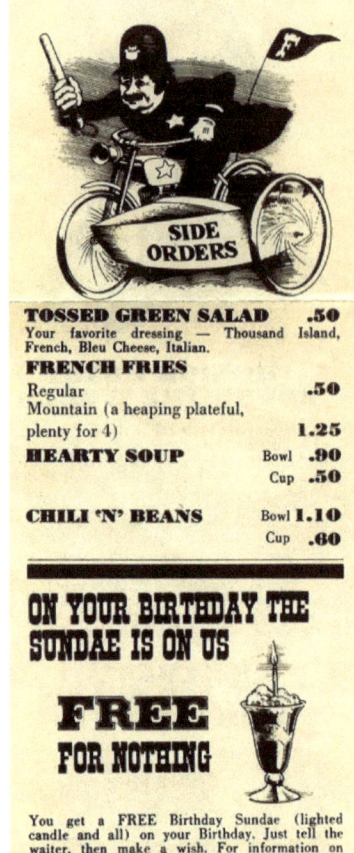

SIDE ORDERS

TOSSED GREEN SALAD .50
Your favorite dressing — Thousand Island, French, Bleu Cheese, Italian.

FRENCH FRIES
Regular .50
Mountain (a heaping plateful, plenty for 4) 1.25

HEARTY SOUP Bowl .90
Cup .50

CHILI 'N' BEANS Bowl 1.10
Cup .60

ON YOUR BIRTHDAY THE SUNDAE IS ON US

FREE FOR NOTHING

You get a FREE Birthday Sundae (lighted candle and all) on your Birthday. Just tell the waiter, then make a wish. For information on our special Birthday parties look on the back of this menu. FUN AND BIRTHDAY PARTIES should only happen at Farrell's!

With thanks and appreciation to John Guest of Christopher's, Inc, Santa Ana, California. John provided high resolution copies of a variety of Farrell's menus to use in this book.

The People – Employees and Customers

Farrell's was both an idea and a concept created and made popular by Bob Farrell. It was a fantastic creation. Bob knew that such a place was missing in the community. It may never have been as successful, or as much fun, if not for the people – the customers and the employees. This combination made it a happening destination, an experience, creating memories to last a lifetime. The following pages include a sample of the hundreds of photographs of the interaction between employees, customers, and management. (Photographs courtesy of John Ortman, Mike Fleming, and others.)

At right, Farrell's,
The shops at Mission Viejo.

Farrell's was all about helping and serving other people. At right, one example is the time they provided ice cream and food booths to benefit a fundraiser for St. Margaret Mary Church in Chino, California.

Farrell's attracted people and fans of all ages. You may even see yourself or someone you know in these photos.

Jeff and Jan Zorn took a trip to the Buena Park Farrell's in 2018, before it closed. With them was Ren and his mom, Jennifer. They not only enjoyed lunch, but Ren explored the candy displays and Jan checked out all the stuffed animals. Sweet Pete's had just updated the candy area. From left, Jennifer, Ren, Jan, and Jeff. (Photos by Jeff Zorn.)

Activities and VIPs

9

In 1978, Farrell's at McCain Mall, N. Little Rock, Arkansas, celebrated George Washington's birthday with a giant birthday sundae. The festivities began February 20 with an ice cream eating contest between Arkansas' then-Attorney General, Bill Clinton and KLAZ-98 radio station's Sonny Victory and Deanna Scott. The winner was Bill Clinton, who reached the bottom of his Pig's Trough first. The sundae was constructed with strawberry topping, cherries, and lots of whipped cream. Everyone sang "Happy Birthday to George," and Bill Clinton blew out the candles and presented the first serving to John Waddle, Arkansas' Muscular Dystrophy poster child. Free ice cream was served to the guests and donation proceeds went to the Muscular Dystrophy Association. (Thanks to Mr. Baker and Farrell's Party Line newsletter June 1978.)

Academy Award winning actor Ernest Borgnine stopped by for some Farrell's ice cream at a pre-Academy Awards event and talked about his trips to Farrell's with his kids. Borgnine had just celebrated his 93rd birthday and, of course, got the Farrell's Famous Happy Birthday Song from Farrell's executives, Courtney, Vickie, and Steve! Borgnine won the 1956 Best Actor Oscar for *Marty*. He will be remembered for McHale's Navy and many other appearances. He passed away in 2012. (March 2010 Farrell's Facebook post.)

Farrell's CEO Michael Fleming and his wife Robbin got to meet Donnie (left) and Marie Osmond (right), siblings pop singing duo and variety television stars. The two are "wonderful Farrell's fans" per Mike. Donnie told Mike he "can't remember how many Pig's Troughs he ate growing up." Marie added "yeah, he's a real pig. LOL" They made plans to attend the next Farrell's grand opening. (Courtesy Michael Fleming and Farrell's USA.)

Left, Hubert Humphrey plays the piano just as President Harry Truman had done. Humphrey was visiting Farrell's during his campaign for the Presidency in 1972. Above, Hubert Humphrey works the fountain while sampling his work. "Once you've worked behind a fountain, you never lose your touch." Humphrey served as Vice President under President Lyndon Johnson 1965-1969; US Senator from Minnesota 1949-1964 and 1971-1976. In 1972, Humphrey ran for the Democratic nomination for President but lost to McGovern. McGovern would lose to Nixon in the Presidential election November 1972. (Farrell's, March 1972.)

Host Mike Douglas, left, presents the World's Largest Ice Cream Sundae to thirty million television viewers as Totie Fields, Bob Farrell, singer Tommy Leonetti, comedian Pat Butram (hidden) and author Paul Dickson admire Farrell's awesome concoction. Image on right, Bob Farrell directs the serving of the sundae. (Courtesy of Kristie Farrell Booster.)

Jennifer Granholm was a teenager when she worked at the San Mateo, California Farrell's. She recalled to me: "I worked there while a high school student, both behind the fountain making sundaes and as a waitress serving huge "zoo's" to kids' birthday parties. It was a hoot— a fun atmosphere and a wholesome job for a teenager. We did not wear t-shirts back then — we wore striped puffy sleeved shirts reminiscent of the 20's, complete with straw hats and arm garters." Granholm would then appear as a contestant on "The Dating Game" and wore her Farrell's uniform shirt on the show.

Jennifer Granholm was destined to go on to bigger and better things. Granholm would be elected Michigan's Attorney General (1999 to 2003), Governor (2003-2011), and has served as the 16th US Secretary of Energy since 2021. (Photo by U.S. Department of Energy.)

This cartoon was published in the Detroit Free Press, May 1974 in an article by Billy Bowles. It described the effort by Farrell's to surpass the then-Guiness record sundae weighing 1,551 pounds which was served on July 4, 1972, in Wooster, Ohio. The planned 2,054-pound sundae ("Definitely Not for Dieters"), with 1,522 pounds (12,600 scoops) of vanilla, 290 pounds of chocolate topping, 35 pounds of sprinkles, 140 pounds of strawberry topping, and 65 pounds of whipped cream. It was 2,053.9 pounds in total and 12 feet high in a special glass sundae dish. Servings were sold for fifty cents to support recreation programs. In the years that followed there have been many other attempts and successes in the largest, and longest sundaes across the U. S. (Courtesy of the Detroit Free Press.)

Farrell's gave America the longest banana split at the 1973 St. Paul, Minnesota Winter Carnival. Record-setting at the time and more than 1.2 miles long!

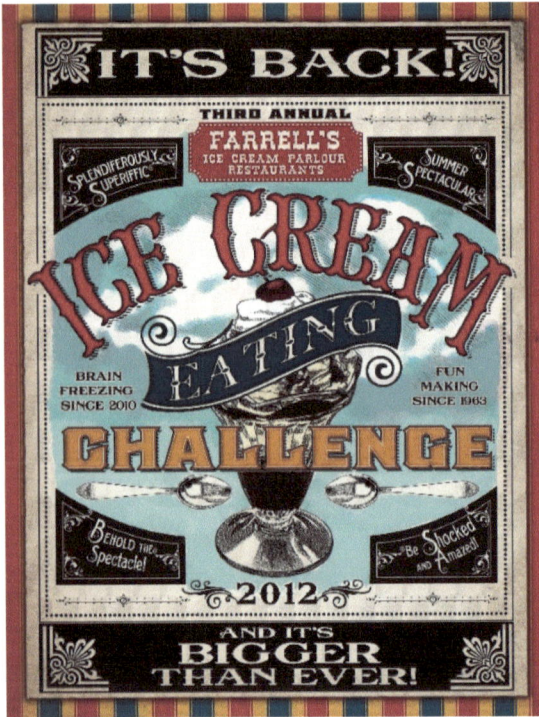

Farrell's held unique events and programs from Ice Cream Eating contests, participating in parades and festivals, and charitable & community donations at various locations.

Mother Goose parades in the 1970s were the largest parade in San Diego County and Farrell's was well-represented with employees marching with pride. "The Mother Goose Parade is San Diego's East County's annual holiday kick-off celebration featuring whimsical floats, clowns, bands," and more. (San Diego.org. Photo courtesy of Mike Fleming, John Ortman.)

Farrell's is well-represented with this distinctive Zoo Fantasy float in the 1970 Rose Parade in Portland, Oregon.

The coupon below was included with the Ice Cream Sodas and Lollipops albums, below left. More about the album on the next page. (Author's collection.)

While beginning to author this book, I remembered a song about Ice Cream Sodas and Lollipops from the 1970s. The more I researched, I found this album that looked like a Farrell's Candy shop. I tracked down Harley Hatcher, the producer and agent for Paul Delicato. Harley gave me the story – Indeed, the Farrell's in Woodland Hills, California on Canoga Avenue, was down the block from Harley's office, and they had a photo shoot for his song, "Ice cream sodas and lollipops." The song quickly became a Billboard chart top ten record, peaking at #7 in October 1975. Harley's "Artists of America Records enjoyed immediate success with the song *Ice Cream Sodas & Lollipops & A Red Hot Spinning Top*, a song written by Harley and performed by Paul Delicato. Delicato enjoyed further success with six Billboard charting records including his biggest hit, *Cara Mia*, which peaked at #5 on Billboard's Adult Contemporary chart. And Farrell's Ice Cream Parlours was the backdrop for this fantastic memory and part of history! (From the author's collection. Thanks to Harley Hatcher for sharing his time!)

This hit song came out in 1975 and was popular during the Bicentennial celebration of July 4, 1976. This song and the message resonate even today! Paul asks, "where did all the people go of yesteryear?" … about "the good old days when deals were made with a handshake…of knowing our neighbors for miles around…of picnics on Sunday afternoons, of laughter... how-do-you-do's…and kindly ways. (amersongmusic and Harley Hatcher.)

Harley Hatcher, award-winning songwriter and producer, with his 1956 Martin guitar, model 00-17 he used to write the hit "Ice Cream Sodas…" (Courtesy of Harley. See HarleyHatcher.com for more information.)

Above, Tommy Lasorda, long-time manager of the Los Angeles Dodgers (1976-1996; 1997 Hall of Fame) spoke to a Little League team at the Buena Park store. According to CEO Mike Fleming, "Tommy was asked to stop there by a friend of a friend of his. He spoke to the kids more about life than baseball." Mike added that, "meeting Tommy that day started a friendship between me and Tom, and his wife Jo. When I went to his house, I would always bring them a Pig's Trough. Tom loved ice cream!" (Photos courtesy of Mike Fleming.)

Above, Farrell's Buena Park CEO Mike Fleming (L) thanks Tommy Lasorda for his encouraging words to the kids.

Barry Goldwater (far right) enjoys a treat as he visits one of the Arizona Farrell's restaurants with friends. Goldwater was a United States Senator (1969-1987) at the time of this visit. (Courtesy of the Ortman collection.)

Jeff Dunham celebrated his 8th birthday with friends at Farrell's in 1970. Jeff recounted the excitement he and his friends shared as the Farrell's staff carried "The Zoo" to his table. Running around the restaurant to the sounds of sirens and cheers from everyone, the staff members tripped and the contents of "Jeff's Zoo" went flying before it reached his table. It may have been very embarrassing for the staff, but it was a memory to last a lifetime for Jeff Dunham and his friends.

Jeff Dunham, who at the age of 9 received his first toy ventriloquist dummy for Christmas, went on to perform and entertain audiences at Kiwanis clubs and banquets in high school and while attending Baylor University. Jeff would become an internationally acclaimed comedian and ventriloquist. According to Slate magazine, Jeff is considered "America's favorite comedian."

Dunham has "nine record-breaking comedy specials to his credit – two were Comedy Central's most viewed specials of their respective years (*Minding the Monsters*, 2012 and *Controlled Chaos*, 2011). Jeff Dunham's *Very Special Christmas Special* in 2008 remains the network's highest rated program of all time. With 5 million YouTube subscribers and 13 million Facebook followers, Jeff has amassed over a billion views and sold over nine million DVDs. Dunham was Billboard's Top Comedy Tour three years in a row." (Courtesy of Jeff Dunham, JeffDunham.com/about.)

Jeff Dunham has been a huge fan of Farrell's since he was 8 years old.

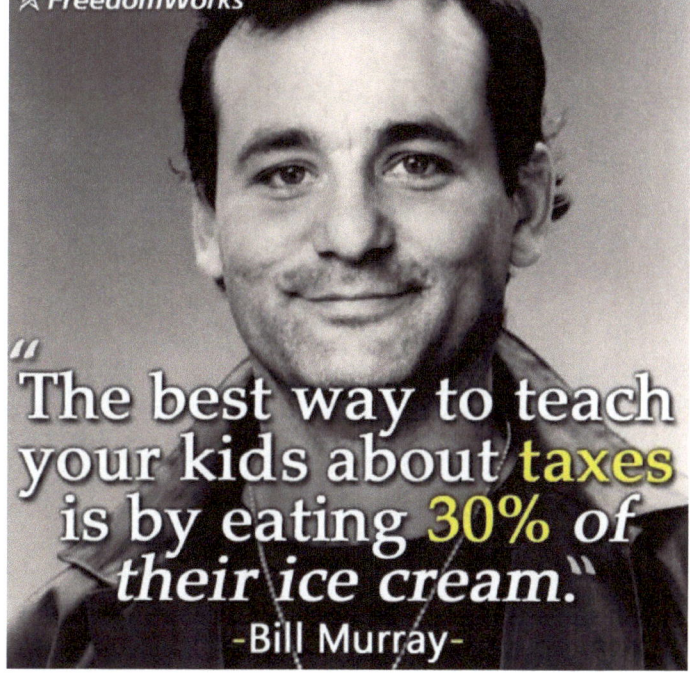

Farrell's sponsored many fundraisers and special events over the years, and some even at their restaurants. The event at left, held at Riverside and Rancho Cucamonga, was to benefit the families of Officer Michael Crain, Detective Jeremiah MacKay, and Deputy Alex Collins. Crain and MacKay were shot and killed by an ex-LAPD officer in 2013. Detective MacKay was shot and killed when he was trying to apprehend the suspect wanted for killing Officer Crain. Collins was shot four times and survived, crediting his partners for saving his life that day. The hunt for the ex-officer was called "the largest manhunt in Southern California history." Proceeds also benefited two police associations.

It's A Tough Job And We Appreciate All You Do!

As a sweet thank you to all fire, police and sheriff personnel in our cities, Farrell's Ice Cream Parlours will offer it's famous two scoop Thank You Sundae free to active firefighters and law enforcement officers now through December 20, 2015.

Valid at participating Farrell's locations. ID is required. For complete details visit FarrellsUSA.com.

From Tragedy Comes Help and Hope

The Farrell's Ice Cream Parlour family experienced three notable tragedies over the years, and at separate locations.

On September 24, 1972, a privately owned Canadair Sabre jet failed to take off while leaving the Golden West Sport Aviation Air Show at Sacramento, California's Executive Airport. It went off the end of the runway and crashed into the Farrell's Ice Cream Parlour. Twenty-two people died and twenty-eight were injured.

On April 9, 1982, a small private plane crashed into the road and burst into flames in front of the Farrell's location in Torrance, California. The pilot and his two passengers died; no one on the ground was harmed.

In April 2014, an out-of-control automobile ran into a line of patrons waiting outside the Buena Park, California location of Farrell's. One person died and six others were injured.

(From Wikipedia and the Sacramento Bee.)

This memorial plaque was dedicated on March 15, 2003, to the victims of the 1972 accident in loving memory of the children and adults, in what was at that time the worst air-ground disaster in our country's history, as noted on the plaque.

This memorial was built in 2002 at the site of the accident (now part of Freeport Square Shopping Center) consisting of a rose garden with two benches, a fountain, a concrete marker, and two metal plaques with the names of those who died. (From The Sacramento Bee, 2014.)

In 2022, a service to commemorate the 50th anniversary was held to remember the victims of the accident.

"Joni Perrin places flowers as her sister Carol Conyers touches the name of their lost sister, Nancy Ann Rodriguez, who was 8 years old when she died with 22 others at the Farrell's Ice Cream Parlour near Executive Airport on September. 24, 1972. One of two plaques bearing names of the people killed in the incident. Twenty-five others were injured." (Allen Pierleoni, Sacramento Bee)

In an article originally published in the December 31, 1999, Sacramento Bee, and modified in 2012, it was described as a "lovely Sunday afternoon in September 1972, as a bunch of kids from the Sacramento 49ers youth football team were celebrating a dad's birthday party at Farrell's Ice Cream Parlour on Freeport Boulevard when their world came to an end. A plane leaving the air show crashed into the ice cream parlour, causing an explosion and fireball that turned 'The Happy Place,' as the parlour was known, into a smoldering tomb. The plane smashed into a corner window of Farrell's, killing twenty-two people, 12 of them children. Another 25 people were injured. Warren Krier, there to celebrate his 32nd birthday was killed, along with his wife, Sandra, and their two children, Jennifer 8, and 2-year-old Brandon, along with their best friend, Tony Martin, and his wife and three children." (By Stephen Magagnini, SacBee.)

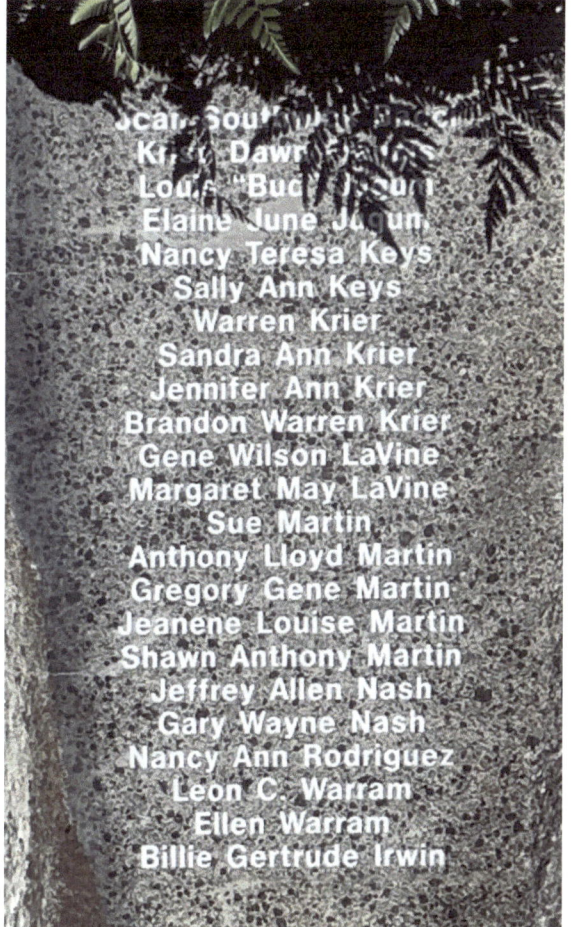

With thanks and appreciation to Rachel Crowell, Director of the Firefighters Burn Institute, Sacramento, California, for forwarding the monument images on the previous pages, along with the Mission Statement, at right. Please consider a donation to these two organizations: The Firefighters Burn Institute and the Regional Burn Center at UC Davis. Their addresses and that of the Memorial Site, all in Sacramento, are displayed on the next page. Thank you.

> **Mission Statement**
>
> The Firefighters Burn Institute is a non-profit 501(c)(3) organization founded by Sacramento Fire Captain Cliff Haskell and the Sacramento Area Fire Fighters Local 522 in 1973, for the purpose of establishing a local burn treatment facility; providing recovery programs for burn survivors; providing fire and burn prevention through public education; funding education for burn team professionals, firefighters, and burn survivors; and supporting burn treatment and rehabilitation research.

Tragedy raised burn awareness

Allen Pierleoni authored this article for the Sacramento Bee. It was originally published Monday, September 24, 2012, and later modified. It describes the efforts and dedication to help others.

"One of the positive things to emerge in the aftermath was the Firefighters Burn Institute.

Sacramento firefighters had been trying to establish a burn-treatment center prior to it but couldn't get traction.

As victims were removed from Farrell's and taken to hospitals, it became agonizingly clear that Sacramento lacked sufficient burn-treatment facilities to deal with such a catastrophe.

Soon afterward, Sacramento Fire Department Capt. Cliff Haskell and Firefighters Local 522 went on a fund-raising mission. The institute was dedicated on December 21, 1973.

"The community needed it because there were no hospital beds available for burn (treatment) at that time, and we firefighters needed it for ourselves, too," said Haskell.

Though the institute has functioned as a "living memorial" to those who perished, its impact has extended beyond the city.

"The comprehensive burn care and advanced research we are doing is enhancing the quality of life for burn survivors throughout the world," said Dr. David Greenhalgh, chief of staff for burn surgery at Shriners Hospitals for Children Northern California and chief of the burn division at neighboring UC Davis Medical Center.

"We are a charitable institution that works closely with Shriners Hospitals for Children and UC Davis Medical Center."

(Allen Pierleoni, Sacramento Bee Published: Monday, Sep. 24, 2012, as modified.)

FIREFIGHTERS BURN INSTITUTE

3101 Stockton Blvd. Sacramento, California 95820 www.ffburn.org

Donations may be made to the Firefighters Burn Institute, at left, or the Burn Center, below. Thank you.

Burn Center: Firefighters Burn Institute Regional Burn Center at UC Davis Health, 2315 Stockton Blvd., Sacramento, California 95817

Memorial Site: City of Sacramento Public Safety Center, 5770 Freeport Blvd., Sacramento, Blvd., Sacramento, California 95822

Sacramento Bee reporter Stephen Magagnini described in his column the actions of one of the Police Officers on scene. "Of all the heroes who stepped up that tragic afternoon, none was more worthy than Sacramento Police Officer Derald R. Landberg. Time and again, Landberg entered the burning building to rescue women and children, then led firefighters through the intense heat and smoke to trapped victims. Finally, he helped a volunteer doctor tend to the injured in the makeshift infirmary outside the building.

Landberg, who is credited with saving a dozen people, was only the second officer in the history of the Sacramento Police Department to receive the Gold Medal of Valor. (Published December 31, 1999, and modified September 6, 2012.)

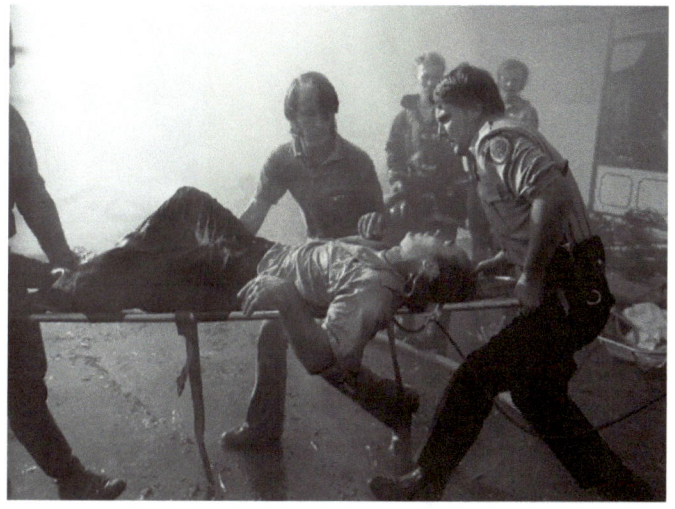

Firefighters and Police Officer rescue survivors of the Farrell's air accident (Leo Neibaur, Sacramento Bee Staff Photo.)

Farrell's CEO, Mike Fleming, recently told me about two grandparents who drove to Farrell's after hearing of the plane crash knowing that their grandchildren had gone there for ice cream. While running across the street to Farrell's, wrongly believing the grandchildren were inside, the grandmother was hit and killed. The kids had left before the plane crash.

"The crash, which wasn't the first in neighborhoods around Executive Airport, forced the closure of the runway to jets, led to a land-use plan for the surrounding area and resulted in a $5 million out-of-court settlement for the survivors and relatives of those who died." (By Stephen Magagnini, Sacramento Bee, December 31, 1999, as modified.)

According to the Sacramento Bee, "twenty-two people died, including twelve children. An eight-year-old survivor of the accident lost nine family members: both parents, two brothers, a sister, two grandparents and two cousins. A family of four also died in the accident. The crash could have claimed many more lives if the external fuel tanks had not ruptured prior to impact, or if the jet had not been slowed by hitting the moving car and other vehicles parked in front of the restaurant. Bingham, the pilot, suffered a broken leg and a broken arm." (Sacramento Bee and Wikipedia.)

At right, "smashed cars lay in ruins in the parking lot of Farrell's Ice Cream Parlor. The cause of the damage is seen in the background. The remains of an F-86 aircraft protrude from the inside of Farrell's Ice Cream Parlor September 24, 1972." (Harlin Smith, Sacramento Bee Staff Photo.)

Farrell's crash, 9/24/1972. (Sacramento Bee Staff Photo, Richard Gilmore.)

Crowds view the tragic scene at Farrell's Ice Cream Parlor Restaurant September 25, 1972. (Sacramento Bee / Richard Gilmore)

April 9, 1982 - "A firefighter hoses the remains of a single-engine aircraft that crashed into a city street in front of the Farrell's Ice Cream Parlour in Torrance, California where a group of children were celebrating a birthday party. At least three people were killed in the crash, according to police." Roger Baker told me that he obtained this image many years ago. "This was my store. I was there in 1985, and this plane crash was April 9, 1982. When I was there, there was still an "X" painted in front of the store, on Hawthorne Blvd., where the plane hit. A memorial of sorts." (Courtesy of Roger Baker, AP)

The Orange County Register reported an accident that happened at the Farrell's Ice Cream Parlour in Buena Park. Reporter Joseph Pimentel wrote that "An elderly driver attempting to park at the restaurant accidentally stepped on the gas pedal instead of the brake and drove over the parking curb and hit people waiting in line. 71-year-old Marisa Malin was killed. Five others were hurt with injuries ranging from a fractured skull, broken ankles, and another with scratches." A state law was introduced because of the accident that aims to "prevent injuries when vehicles crash into businesses. The bill was intended to encourage commercial building owners to install protective barriers to separate parking lots from buildings." Michael Fleming, CEO of Parlour Enterprises which owned the restaurant at the time, said, "This is the right thing to do. But I don't think it does enough." The article went on to say that Fleming hosted a press conference at the restaurant to champion the bill and to thank first responders. According to the article, "Fleming would prefer the barriers are mandatory, but sees this as a step toward his goal." (Photographs of the car accident provided by Mike Fleming, CEO of Farrell's, with additional thanks for the news coverage by KCAL2 News/CBS Los Angeles.)

The Marriott Years

Marriott Corporation purchased the Farrell's chain in June 1972. This new acquisition for the company began with "24 company-owned and 40 franchised units, mostly in the Mid-West and Western U.S.," according to the 1972 Marriott Annual Report. Through the next decade Marriott would add more company-owned and franchised units. The Farrell's name grew in popularity while sales and profits almost doubled in the early years. Sales for Farrell's in 1971 were $4.5 million. Farrell's Ice Cream Parlour Restaurants – A great food experience. (Images on these pages are courtesy of Marriott International Corporate Archives and The University of Houston Libraries Digital Collections.)

"Everyone has a good time at Farrell's, now a part of Marriott Restaurant Operations and spreading its network of 'ice cream parlour restaurants' from the West Coast to the East!" (1972 Marriott Corporation Annual Report.)

Prior to the printing of the 1972 Annual Report, Restaurant Operations Group President G. Michael Hostage was asked by investment community security analysts how Farrell's fit into the Marriott plan. Michael Hostage stated that, "Farrell's is the most exciting chain of family-oriented fun-and-food facilities in the United States. About ten years ago founder Bob Farrell built an ice cream parlour around the Gay Nineties theme, offered quality food, humor, bright colors, a player piano, singing, sirens, drums – and made it a real 'experience' for the customer. From that beginning in Portland, Oregon, he built Farrell's into 24 company-owned units and 40 franchised units and launched a national concept. An outstanding success story – one we like to identify with."

Farrell's grows in popularity, and expansion is stepped up. In 1973, six new units were opened, including the first ones on the East Coast starting in the Washington, D.C. area. "The total in operation rose to 30, and expansion plans are ambitious for fiscal '74 and beyond," according to company officials. Robert E. "Bob" Farrell is listed in the Corporate Officers – President, Farrell's Division Restaurant Operations in the Annual Reports. (Annual Report.)

"Spectacular ice cream treats highlight a varied menu offered with fun and flair – the most unique such operation in America." (1973 Marriott Corporation Annual Report.)

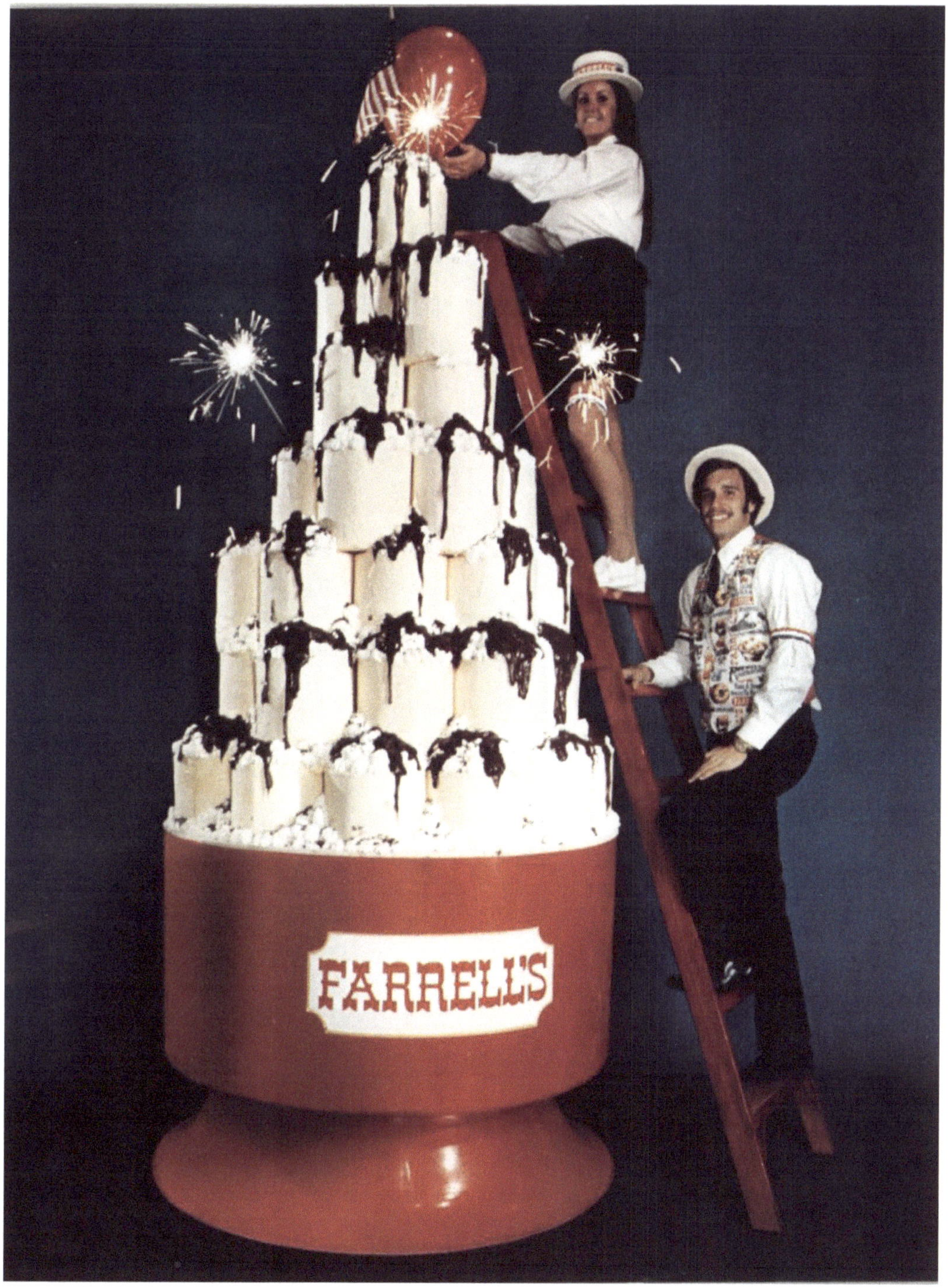

Building the "World's Largest Sundae" for special events by Farrell's and spreading the fun nationwide. Farrell's Ice Cream Parlour Restaurant sales and profits were almost double the year before. The number of company-owned units doubled in fiscal '74 by acquisition of 16 franchised units in Los Angeles and the state of Washington, and by opening 14 new locations. "We now have 60 Parlours and are beginning to span the continent, achieving national recognition for Farrell's famous brand of wholesome fun and great ice cream specialties." (1974 Marriott Corporation Annual Report.)

"Farrell's acceptance by the public everywhere has been outstanding. It is a concept we intend to expand aggressively – a 42% growth in number of units is programmed for fiscal 1975." (1974 Marriott Corporation Annual Report.)

Farrell's Restaurant division achieved its planned expansion in 1975, insuring more prime market positioning for this unique fun and food concept. Sales growth far outpaced the rate of unit expansion, but profits declined as the division absorbed start-up costs for 23 new parlours, including 6 acquired units. Entering new geographic areas also required additional advertising and supervisory expense. Traffic in the new year picked up generally as a growing number of consumers visited shopping malls where most Farrell's parlours were located.

**This is Marriott Farrell's ... 1975
(Restaurants Across the U.S.)**

Parlour Restaurants	83
Franchised Operations	22

"A dozen more Farrell's are planned in fiscal 1976 and the additions are expected to help keep the division growing long-term. The slower expansion will cut opening costs sharply. Profits should benefit in fiscal 1976 from the full effects of last year's new unit expansion and improved operating controls recently adopted." (1975 Marriott Corporation Annual Report.)

Marriott Corporation's 1977 Annual Report noted that the Restaurant Operations suffered from the coldest winter in the history of the company. "Increasing losses in the Farrell's Ice Cream Parlour division made it an especially difficult first half. But profits improved in most divisions in the second half."

FARRELL'S RESTAURANTS

Farrell's broke even in the last quarter of fiscal '77. But for the full year, losses were substantially greater than in '76 when the division first became unprofitable.

Increased labor and food costs had a serious impact, and customer counts were a problem. Also, expenses were incurred by the division as it concluded its management reorganization, relocated its division base to Washington, D.C. and deployed a Group-wide task force to improve operations.

New efficiencies from improved manpower scheduling and controls are having a good impact. Marketing efforts are being emphasized. And Farrell's Ice Cream Parlour Restaurants should show a marked improvement in fiscal '78.

In the 1978 Annual Report, Farrell's had 83 locations in 22 States. Farrell's successful rebound from its 1976 loss carried into '78 and further profit improvement was projected for 1979. A number of these ice cream parlour restaurants had been closed or sold as franchise operations, and division cost control programs proved their effectiveness.

Farrell's was a bright spot in 1979. It reported another excellent profit gain for the third straight year. The division continued to strengthen operations in satisfactory markets and eliminated several unprofitable locations. There were 77 ice cream parlour restaurants — down from 89 two years ago. However, during the next two years, Marriott officials would review how Farrell's fit into their long-term plans.

Above, the front cover of Marriott Corporation's 1979 Annual Report. The images, including Farrell's sundae at the bottom, display just some of the 13 separate businesses, demonstrating the diversification and the strength of the renowned Marriott name. At left, servers prepare a variety of sundaes.

On March 9, 1982, Marriott completed its sale of Farrell's Ice Cream Parlour Restaurant Division to a group of private investors for $15,000,000 plus $1,886,000 for inventories. Farrell's sales and operating income for 1982 through the disposition date were $8,376,000 and $970,000 (including gain on sale), and were $50,531,000 and $3,646,000 for 1981, and $51,646,000 and $2,770,000 for 1980. Officers said, "this sale is consistent with the decision to concentrate efforts of the Restaurant Group primarily in the fast food and coffee shop market segments." (1982 Marriott Corporation Annual Report.)

Marcus Lemonis
"The Profit" TV Show
The Auction of Memorabilia

By August 2016 there were four remaining Farrell's Ice Cream stores: Riverside, Buena Park, Brea, and Santa Clarita. The Sacramento and Rancho Cucamonga locations had closed. Riverside, Buena Park, and Brea would remain open, but only temporarily. Riverside closed in 2017 with the contents from the store, inside and out, auctioned off. I was the winning bidder on a variety of items.

On August 23, 2016, after extensive tapings, the first Episode of Season 4 of the television show, *The Profit,* with host Marcus Lemonis, featured Farrell's Ice Cream Parlours. Marcus Lemonis is an American businessman, television personality and philanthropist. He is known for his role as the star of *The Profit,* a CNBC reality show about saving small businesses.

Lemonis met with partners Mike Fleming and Paul Kramer, and their staff to review operations and arrange to purchase a 51% ownership. A second program called "Fighting for Farrell's" would air February 27, 2018. Buena Park would close soon after, on December 30, 2018. Brea, owned by private investors and not Lemonis, would close on June 8, 2019, leaving no remaining Farrell's locations.

Thanks to the people at CNBC / NBC Universal and the production company for *The Profit*, Machete Productions for the licensing agreement and permission to use the images from the show. (Marcus Lemonis in front of the Rancho Cucamonga location after meeting with staff. Marcus Lemonis, *The Profit*, and TV Guide)

Above left, and right, Marcus walks into Farrell's Rancho Cucamonga for the first time and ponders what improvements need to be made, while CEO Mike Fleming watches from the side. Below, left, Marcus reviews the results of using a new pizza recipe with Farrell's Rancho Cucamonga GM Travis Lee and marketing director, Shauna Parisi. Below, right, Marcus asks Sandy Gruzdis why she was against Shauna's ideas for making display changes while Shauna Parisi looks on.

Below, left, Marcus tells General Manager Travis Lee about the change to have Shauna Parisi oversee merchandise and candy purchasing. Right, Marcus, listening to a birthday announcement by the Farrell's servers.

Below, left, Marcus listens to marketing director, Shauna Parisi, as she tells him about products in the candy shop that should be eliminated. Sandy Gruzdis, HR and Purchasing Director listens. Below, right, Marcus and Shauna.

The Auction of Memorabilia

They closed Riverside and auctioned the items in September 2017. Everything had to go from inside and outside of the store. The nearly five hundred lots included pencils and postcards, umbrellas, t-shirts, drums, lamps, and even the Statue of Liberty that was near the front lobby.

The Buena Park store closed for remodeling and renovations and reopened in August 2017. However, after an attempt by Marcus Lemonis to turn a profit and save it, it was closed on December 30, 2018. The host of CNBC'S reality business show *"The Profit"* spent months shooting there in 2016. The Brea store was privately owned by a group of investors. On June 8, 2019, Brea, the last of the Farrell's Ice Cream Parlours closed, apparently signaling the end of the chain. (With appreciation to I-15 auctions.)

Johan Graham, co-owner of I-15 Auctions, shows items that were sold in an online auction at Farrell's Ice Cream Parlour in Riverside on Friday, Sept. 8, 2017. (Photo by Watchara Phomicinda, The Press-Enterprise/SCNG.)

The following pages show just a few of the thousands of items that were offered in the auction. Some of these items are now in my collection. With appreciation to co-owner, Johan Graham and staff, Amy Stark, Tari Blalock, and CEO Jeff Patterson of I-15 Auctions in California. They helped coordinate the shipment of my items (in a photo on a pallet, ready to be shipped to me) and provided photographs of hundreds of items, many of which appear on the following pages. It is sad to see they can no longer provide smiles and enjoyment to future generations, but glad that I, and many others, were able to take advantage of preserving some of the memories.

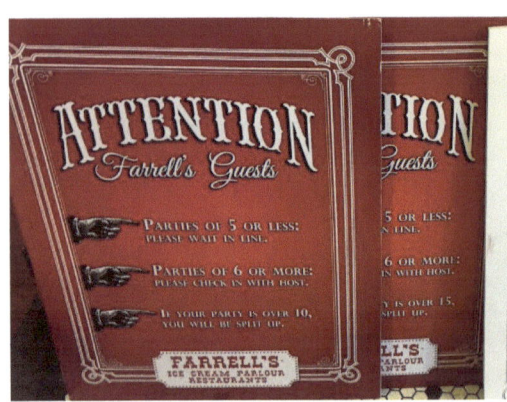  

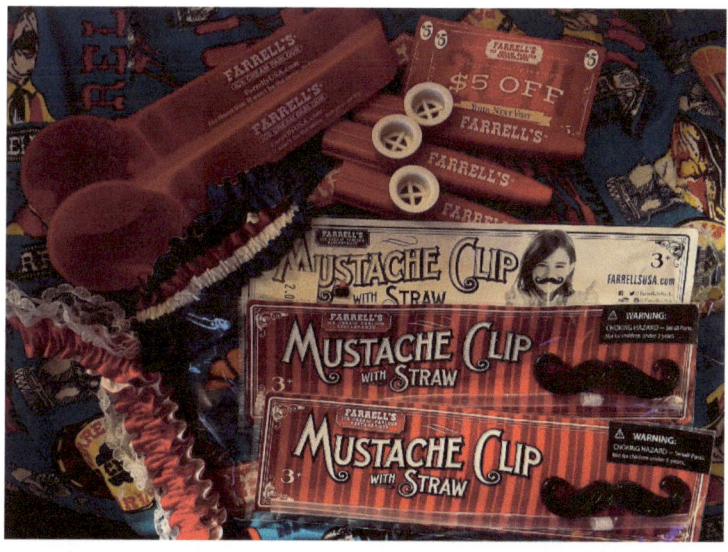

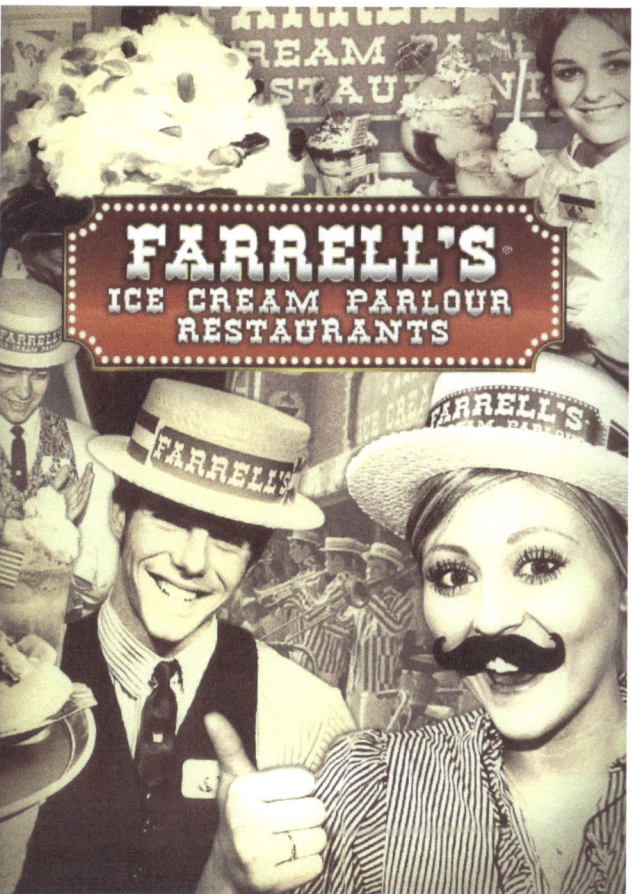

www.ingramcontent.com/pod-product-compliance
Lightning Source LLC
Chambersburg PA
CBHW041536220426
43663CB00002B/49